MORMONISM

THE BASICS

Although often regarded as marginal or obscure, Mormonism is a significant American religious minority, both numerically and politically. The successes and struggles of this U.S.-born religion reveal much about how religion operates in U.S. society. *Mormonism: The Basics* introduces the teachings, practices, evolution, and internal diversity of this movement, whose cultural icons range from Mitt Romney to the *Twilight* saga, from young male missionaries in white shirts and ties to polygamous women in pastel prairie dresses.

This is the first introductory text on Mormonism that tracks not only the mainstream LDS but also two other streams within the movement – the liberalized RLDS and the polygamous Fundamentalists – thus showing how Mormons have pursued different approaches to defining their identity and their place in society. The book addresses these questions:

- Are Mormons Christian, and why does it matter?
- How have Mormons worked out their relationship to the state?
- How have Mormons diverged in their thinking about gender and sexuality?
- How do rituals and regulations shape Mormon lives?
- What types of sacred spaces have Mormons created?
- What strategies have Mormons pursued to establish a global presence?

Mormonism: The Basics is an ideal introduction for anyone wanting to understand this religion within its primarily American but increasingly globalized contexts.

David J. Howlett is a visiting assistant professor of religion at Skidmore College in Saratoga Springs, New York, USA.

John-Charles Duffy is a lecturer in comparative religion at Miami University in Oxford, Ohio, USA.

D1452502

THE BASICS

MORMONISM

THE BASICS

David J. Howlett and
John-Charles Duffy

Routledge
Taylor & Francis Group

LONDON AND NEW YORK

First published 2017
by Routledge
2 Park Square, Milton Park, Abingdon, Oxon OX14 4RN

and by Routledge
711 Third Avenue, New York, NY 10017

Routledge is an imprint of the Taylor & Francis Group, an informa business

© 2017 David J. Howlett and John-Charles Duffy

British Library Cataloguing in Publication Data
A catalogue record for this book is available from the British Library

Library of Congress Cataloging in Publication Data
Names: Duffy, John-Charles, 1972– author. | Howlett, David James, 1978– author.
Title: Mormonism : the basics / by John-Charles Duffy and David J. Howlett.
Description: New York, NY : Routledge, 2016. | Includes bibliographical references and index.
Identifiers: LCCN 2016019238 (print) | LCCN 2016020438 (ebook) | ISBN 9781138020474 (alk. paper) | ISBN 9781315453972
Subjects: LCSH: Church of Jesus Christ of Latter-day Saints—Doctrines. | Community of Christ—Doctrines. | Mormon fundamentalism. | Mormon Church—Doctrines. | Church of Jesus Christ of Latter-day Saints—History. | Community of Christ—History. | Mormon Church—History.
Classification: LCC BX8635.3 .D84 2016 (print) | LCC BX8635.3 (ebook) | DDC 289.3—dc23
LC record available at https://lccn.loc.gov/2016019238

ISBN: 978-1-138-02047-4 (hbk)
ISBN: 978-1-138-02048-1 (pbk)
ISBN: 978-1-315-45397-2 (ebk)

Typeset in Bembo and Scala Sans
by Apex CoVantage, LLC

To my niece and nephews –

Allie, Ethan, and Timothy,

the next generation of their religious tradition
– DJH

To my mother
– JCD

CONTENTS

FIGURES

INTRODUCTION

The beginning of the twenty-first century saw a surge of media interest in Mormonism. The surge started when the 2002 Winter Olympics were hosted in Salt Lake City, headquarters of Mormonism's largest denomination, the Church of Jesus Christ of Latter-day Saints (LDS Church for short). Mormons kept appearing in the news in the years that followed, as state and federal governments cracked down on polygamists accused of sex with underage teens; as the LDS Church experienced a backlash for its support of a high-profile campaign to ban same-sex marriage in California; and as Mormon politician Mitt Romney ran for U.S. president, first in 2008, then again in 2012. Every time you turned around, Mormons were popping up somewhere in the media: in documentaries and reality TV, game shows, political punditry, *Oprah*, *South Park*, *Big Love*, *Angels in America*, the *Twilight* saga, *The Book of Mormon* musical.

Mormonism is a puzzle. On the one hand, it is one of the United States' more significant religious minorities, numerically and politically speaking. In 2012, the LDS Church was ranked as the fourth largest religious body in the United States, after Catholics, Southern Baptists, and United Methodists. A 2014 survey reported that the U.S. population contained nearly as many Mormons as Jews, and twice as many Mormons as Muslims. Mormons form an important political force in the Intermountain West. They're also well represented in the federal government, where, for example, Mormon Democrat Harry Reid of Nevada served as Senate majority leader during the same years that Mormon Republican and former Massachusetts governor Mitt Romney was running for president. Mormons, it seems, are all around, and they're helping to run the country.

And yet — here's the other hand — Mormons are often regarded as obscure and marginal. Both of the authors of this book have had the experience of teaching students who told us they were interested in knowing more about Mormonism because they'd had Mormon friends but didn't know much about their religion (and evidently hesitated to ask). What Americans do know, or think they know, about Mormons, they appear not to like. Sociologists have found that Mormons are one of the religious groups toward whom Americans feel most negatively: only Muslims and atheists are more disliked. Judging from the recent media representations, Mormons are widely perceived as strange. They believe odd things, so it goes, like God living on a planet called Kolob or Native Americans being a lost tribe of Jews. They wear "magic underwear." They won't drink caffeine. There's uncertainty over whether or not Mormonism is a kind of Christianity. There's confusion about the relationship between the LDS Church, with its young male missionaries in white shirts and ties, and the polygamist groups whose women wear pastel prairie dresses. Various clouds hang over Mormonism: racism, authoritarianism, allegations of covered-up sexual abuse, gays and lesbians driven to suicide, and a dark history of violence.

So what are the facts about Mormonism? And what does the relative success of this controversial religious minority reveal about how religion works in American society?

ABOUT THIS BOOK

The recent surge of media interest in Mormonism has led to a proliferation of books on the movement. What's different about this one?

First, most books on Mormonism focus on only one branch of Mormonism: the largest branch, the LDS Church. Other branches of the movement, such as the polygamist groups, are treated parenthetically if at all.

By contrast, we present Mormonism as a movement of people who, at every stage of their history, have disagreed over what it means to be Mormon. Such disagreements are a basic reality in any religious movement. Therefore, to have a basic understanding of Mormonism, you need an understanding of the key disagreements among Mormons. If we wrote this book as if all Mormons believe or live their tradition the same way, we would be giving you a false impression of how religious movements operate. We would be describing Mormonism only from the perspective of the victors in the movement's internal struggles.

Throughout this book, then, we will talk about Mormonism as a movement with three diverging streams: (1) the LDS Church; (2) the Reorganization, also known as the RLDS Church; and (3) the Fundamentalists. We will describe these streams and how they diverged in chapter 1. There are other streams within Mormonism besides these three – other branches within the movement. But these three are the ones most likely to cross your path, because of either their size or their notoriety.

A second distinguishing feature of this book is that where other introductions to Mormonism tend to focus on how Mormons *differ* from other people, we believe that it is equally important to show how Mormons *resemble* other people. By doing this, we aim to help you understand aspects of Mormon teaching or practice that might otherwise seem simply bizarre but that, in fact, represent larger trends on the American religious landscape (even if Mormons give those trends highly distinctive twists). We will show you how Mormonism fits into broader contexts from American religious history, and we will point you to comparisons with other religious movements in the United States.

This book, then, introduces you not only to Mormonism but also to frameworks that can help you understand religion in American society more broadly, especially minority religions. In the process of coming to understand Mormonism, you will also gain insight into

- how minority religions relate to America's Christian majority (chapter 2).
- how church–state relations work in the United States (chapter 3).
- how debates over gender and sexuality have developed within American religions (chapter 4).
- how religions organize Americans' daily lives and regulate their behavior (chapter 5).

- how Americans create and use sacred spaces (chapter 6).
- how religious movements forged in the United States adapt to new global cultural settings (chapter 7).

Bear in mind that this book is a *basic* introduction to Mormonism. It offers you a story of Mormonism's diverging streams; an overview of differences in how Mormons interpret their movement's identity and position themselves within society; a sketch of larger contexts useful for making sense of this religion. Other works treat these subjects at greater length, although without tying them all together as we've done. We'll point you to sources you can use to explore further.

A PERSONAL NOTE ABOUT THE AUTHORS

Our scholarly interest in Mormonism is linked to broader interests we have as historians of American religion. But our interest is also personal: each of us has a somewhat unusual Mormon background.

David's parents were Restorationists, former members of the RLDS Church who left because they opposed the ordination of women and other liberalizing changes. Although raised Restorationist, David returned as a young adult to the RLDS Church, now called Community of Christ.

John-Charles's parents were LDS converts. As a young adult, he served a mission for the LDS Church in the Dominican Republic. He was excommunicated from the church after he came out as gay and formed a domestic partnership, now a legal marriage, with an LDS man from Argentina.

A SUGGESTION FOR TEACHERS

Teachers of American religion have grappled for years with the problem of how to organize the introductory survey course. As a grand narrative? A survey of traditions? An exploration of selected themes? The dilemma has been how to preserve chronological or thematic coherence while at the same time doing justice to the United States' expansive religious diversity. In the groundbreaking 1997 anthology *Retelling U.S. Religious History*, Thomas Tweed and his collaborators proposed approaching the dilemma by narrating American religion from multiple vantage points – to see what American religion would look like when viewed from a certain location or through the eyes of a certain group.

In writing *Mormonism: The Basics*, we have taken a cue from Tweed and his collaborators. *Mormonism: The Basics* is not simply an introduction to what Mormons believe and do or to the story of Mormonism. Rather, this book offers readers an introduction to American religion more broadly, through the lens of Mormonism. In other words, Mormonism serves here as a starting point for examining key themes and larger patterns or developments in American religion. Our goal was that *Mormonism: The Basics* could be used in an introductory American religion course as the central, anchoring text, to be extensively supplemented by comparative case studies from other religious movements. Here's how that might work.

Chapter 1 provides an overarching narrative of Mormonism's historical development, which coincides with U.S. religious history from the antebellum period to the present. (For a narrative of U.S. religious history that reaches back to the colonial era, see chapter 2.) A key facet of chapter 1 – and of the entire book – is that it presents Mormonism as a tradition that developed in multiple streams as different groups of Mormons chose different pathways through American culture: the mainstream LDS, the liberalized RLDS, and the polygamous Fundamentalists. *Mormonism: The Basics* thus provides a model to help students recognize the internal diversity and contestation that are basic characteristics of other religious traditions as well. Our recurring contrast, throughout the book, of the LDS to the RLDS offers a framework for discussing the conservative-liberal divide in post-1960s American religion more broadly. Likewise, our discussions of the polygamous Fundamentalist groups offer a framework for discussing the experiences of other marginalized new religious movements (NRMs).

The book's remaining chapters address the following themes: religious pluralism vs. Protestant dominance (chapter 2), church–state relations (chapter 3), gender and sexuality (chapter 4), lived religion (chapter 5), sacred space (chapter 6), and strategies for religious globalization (chapter 7). Each chapter includes some kind of bigger picture that pushes the discussion beyond Mormonism: theoretical concepts, a larger historical narrative for context, or gestures toward comparative cases. Thus, you could use each chapter as the starting point for a short unit on that chapter's theme. You would start the unit by examining the theme in relation to Mormonism. Then, you would extend the discussion over the next few class sessions with supplemental readings that explore the same theme in the experience of other American religious groups. Although we don't dedicate entire chapters to the themes of race or immigration, we do discuss those subjects in relation to Mormonism; we thereby provide jumping-off points for exploring them, too, as themes of broader relevance in U.S. religious history.

A BRIEF HISTORY OF MORMONS

Let's begin your introduction to Mormonism with the basic story: a condensed account of nearly two centuries of Mormon history. Think of this chapter as your map of the general terrain. In later chapters, we'll zoom in to reexamine some portions of the map – some aspects of the story – in greater detail. But this first chapter gives you a picture of how everything fits together.

Over the course of the nineteenth and twentieth centuries, Mormonism grew from a handful of families living in the United States to a family of denominations whose members could be found around the globe. Mormonism was transformed repeatedly as Mormons grappled with changing circumstances: new conflicts within the movement, new sources of opposition from outside, new trends in the larger American society, and new cultural contexts as the movement expanded internationally.

As we move in this chapter from one historical period to the next, we will keep revisiting the following questions:

- How have Mormons gone about forming their religious communities?
- In what ways have Mormons disagreed about what their movement should look like?
- What kind of opposition has Mormonism faced from outsiders?

- How has Mormonism expanded beyond its birthplace in the United States?
- How do major developments in the history of Mormonism relate to larger social trends?

1830–1860: TUMULTUOUS ORIGINS

Mormonism formally began in 1830. Two events mark that beginning. First, a 24-year-old farmer in upstate New York named Joseph Smith Jr. published a Bible-like volume called *The Book of Mormon*. From his teenage years, Smith had experienced visions. Now he claimed that the Book of Mormon was a lost work of ancient scripture, which he had miraculously translated from golden plates that an angel had shown him were buried near his home. The ancient record was supposed to have been written by Israelites who sailed across the ocean in Old Testament times to settle in the Americas; the book contained their prophecies of Jesus's then-future life, death, and resurrection, as well as teachings that Jesus himself gave during a visit he made to the Americas after he rose from the dead.

Smith hadn't worked alone at translating and publishing the Book of Mormon. He had been aided by family and friends who believed that God was inaugurating an important work among them. A few days after the book's publication, a small group of believers gathered for the second event that marks the formal beginning of Mormonism: launching a tiny organization called the Church of Christ, later renamed the Church of Jesus Christ of Latter Day Saints.

JOSEPH SMITH JR.'S FIRST VISION

Smith experienced his first religious vision as a teenager, in the woods near his Palmyra, New York, home. For the earliest Mormons, this vision was less important than Smith's later visions of the angel who led him to the golden plates from which he translated the Book of Mormon. But all Mormon groups today see "the First Vision" as a foundational part of their story. Of several accounts Smith left of that vision, this is the earliest:

. . . I cried unto the Lord for mercy for there was none else to whom I could go and obtain mercy and the Lord heard my cry in the wilderness and while in the attitude of calling upon the Lord a piller of light above the brightness of the sun at noon day come down from above and rested upon me and I was filled with the spirit of god and the Lord opened the heavens upon me and I saw the Lord and he spake unto me saying Joseph my son thy sins are forgiven thee. go thy way walk in my statutes and keep my commandments behold I am the Lord of glory I was crucifyed for the world that all those who believe on my name may have Eternal life behold the world lieth in sin at this time and none doeth good no not one they have turned asside from the gospel and keep not my commandments they draw near to me with their lips while their hearts are far from me and mine anger is kindling against the inhabitants of the earth to visit them according to thir ungodliness and to bring to pass that which hath been spoken by the mouth of the prophets and Apostles behold and lo I come quickly as it written of me in the cloud clothed in the glory of my Father and my soul was filled with love and for many days I could rejoice with great Joy and the Lord was with me but could find none that would believe the hevnly vision . . .

Source: "History, circa Summer 1832," *The Joseph Smith Papers*, josephsmithpapers.org. Spelling, capitalization, and punctuation are reproduced as found in the original manuscript.

Outsiders gave adherents of this new religious movement the nickname Mormons, in reference to the Book of Mormon (which was named, in turn, for one of the ancient prophets whose writings the book was supposed to contain). Adherents called themselves Latter Day Saints – or Latter-day Saints, to use more modern punctuation and capitalization. In calling themselves "Saints," they meant that God had saved them from sin and that they aspired to lead holy lives. The term "latter-day" referred to their belief that they were living in the last days before Jesus's second coming, when evil would be destroyed and God's purposes would be fulfilled.

"Latter-day" had another meaning, too. Mormons regarded their movement as a latter-day, or modern, restoration of the religion founded by Jesus. Jesus's teachings, Mormons believed, had become corrupted over time; but now through new revelations, such as the Book of Mormon, God was restoring Christianity in its purity. Through Mormonism, human beings once again had access to divine powers that had not been fully available on earth for centuries, including the power to properly administer rites that enable people to enter heaven after they die. Mormons understood themselves as called by God to take a message of warning to everyone on earth: people needed to join Christ's true church and form holy communities, where they would be sheltered from the destruction soon to be poured out on the wicked world.

Although Mormonism presented itself as unique, it attracted converts precisely because it reflected wider trends in people's religious tastes. Mormonism appeared at a time when many Americans were looking for religion – and looking for something *new* in religion. Hence, for example, in the early 1800s hundreds of thousands of Americans joined the Methodists, a young Protestant movement whose members formed tight-knit fellowships supporting one another in the pursuit of holy lives. A variety of smaller, unconventional religious movements flourished in the United States during this period as well. Some predicted the imminent end of the world. Some sought to recover the pure, original Christianity of Jesus. Some created experiments in communal living. Some claimed special powers of healing or communication with spirits. Some produced new scriptures. Some embraced unusual sexual norms, ranging from celibacy to free love.

Mormonism offered its own variation on all of these trends in religious innovation. By 1860, tens of thousands of people had chosen a Mormon variation as their preferred religion. Most of these converts were white Americans, but ambitious Mormon missionaries were already working to carry the new religion around the globe: to Britain, Europe, Palestine, South Africa, India, Australia, the Pacific islands, and South America.

Mormon communities grew rapidly during the movement's first three decades; but they did so under severe stress, caused by repeated migrations, internal struggles, and violent conflict with neighbors. When the first Mormons set out to create holy communities, they did so by "gathering" – relocating together to form their own settlements and cities. During the 1830s, Mormons established several communities in Ohio and Missouri. The most important of these, symbolically at least, was located at Independence, Missouri. Joseph Smith Jr. announced a revelation declaring Independence to be the "center place" where Mormons would build Zion, an ideal city from which Jesus would rule when he returned to earth. Part of what would make Zion an ideal city was that its inhabitants would live the "law of consecration," a communitarian system in which they would pool and then redistribute their property to ensure that everyone had enough. In Zion, there would be no poor. Thousands of Mormons migrated to Missouri with plans to implement the law of consecration.

The Mormons' first efforts to build communities in Ohio and Missouri collapsed into crisis. These crises had two causes. The first was internal conflict. Mormonism was constantly changing during the 1830s and early 1840s as Smith kept announcing new visions and revelations, leading to new scriptures, doctrines, rites, and institutions; the Book of Mormon had been just the beginning. (We'll describe the evolution of early Mormonism more fully in chapter 2.) While some Mormons were thrilled by this continual outpouring of new revelations, others became alienated when the movement they had joined evolved into something different. Some Mormons became convinced that Smith had become a "fallen prophet"; some came to regard him as dictatorial; others lost faith in his leadership because of material setbacks that befell the communities. Some of Mormonism's earliest devotees and leaders turned into bitter enemies of the movement. Internal dissension led to the collapse of the Mormons' communities in Ohio after just a few years. Smith and those still loyal to him moved to Missouri to join the Mormon communities there.

The second source of crisis was opposition from outsiders. Some of this opposition came from Protestants who regarded Mormonism as unorthodox and therefore saw its growth as threatening the establishment of a properly Christian America. Protestants opposed various other groups for the same reason, including Catholics, Unitarians, Deists, and Adventists. As soon as Mormonism appeared, Protestant writers denounced it: Smith was a fraud and a tyrant, while his followers were fanatical, superstitious dupes. Additionally, Mormons were perceived as a political threat. As Mormons gathered into a region, the influx of so many newcomers led to friction with neighbors who feared that Mormons would gain political dominance.

Such friction turned bloody in Missouri, which in the 1830s was a battleground state in the nation's escalating conflict over slavery. Fearing that Mormons moving in from northern states would vote to restrict slavery, pro-slavery Missourians tried to drive Mormons out by mob violence. When Mormons held their ground, a small-scale civil war ensued. Finally the governor of Missouri authorized the state militia to "exterminate" the thousands of Mormons living in the state, at which point Mormons fled for their lives. The trauma of the Mormons' expulsion from Missouri was intensified by the fact that they were being driven from Zion, their sacred center place.

Regrouping in Illinois in the 1840s, Mormons founded a new city, Nauvoo, which soon approached the size of Chicago, thanks partly to the immigration of 5,000 converts from Britain. In Nauvoo, Mormons did not attempt to implement the law of consecration, which in Ohio and Missouri had been plagued with difficulties. But the community that Mormons organized in Nauvoo was unusual for a different reason: Nauvoo was a theocracy, where religious and secular government were fused. This was a new development in Mormon community-building. In his capacity as God's prophet *and* ruler of a city, Smith directed all areas of Nauvoo's social life.

As in Ohio and Missouri, so also in Nauvoo, Mormon community collapsed in the face of internal struggle and external violence. Smith's theocratic leadership led to yet another round of alienation and defection among his followers, especially when rumors circulated that Smith and an inner circle were secretly practicing polygamy on the authority of a new revelation. Meanwhile, outsiders feared what they saw as Mormons' fanatical obedience to Smith, Mormons' voting power, and their militia. As the conflict intensified, Smith ordered the destruction of a newspaper produced in Nauvoo by Mormons hostile to his leadership. This action allowed Smith's opponents to bring legal charges against him. He was arrested, then shot to death by a mob.

Following Joseph Smith Jr.'s death in 1844, Mormons were divided not only over the question of who should now lead their movement but what their movement should look like. Some wanted to build on innovations introduced shortly before Smith's death, such as polygamous marriages and secretive rites being performed in the Mormons' newly completed temple at Nauvoo. Other members of the movement wanted to return to earlier, simpler versions of Mormonism. Mormons quickly splintered into competing groups.

About three-fourths of Mormons followed Brigham Young, one of the movement's most prominent missionaries. Young's followers migrated to what is today Utah. We will refer to this stream of Mormonism as the LDS, a standard abbreviation for the Church of Jesus Christ of Latter-day Saints, the name that Young's followers retained. In Utah and surrounding western territories, the LDS greatly extended the impulse to build holy communities: they set out to build not just a holy city but an entire theocratic state, a literal kingdom of God on earth, governed by Young acting as church president and God's prophet.

Almost immediately, however, the Mexican-American War of 1846–1848 turned Utah, which had been a remote part of Mexico, into U.S. territory. As the United States established control over its new territories, the LDS lost their brief independence and chafed under the rule of unwanted outsiders. In 1857, with the rest of the nation moving rapidly toward civil war, federal troops were ordered to Utah out of fear that the LDS might revolt. The LDS, fearing that the U.S. government sought to exterminate them as Missouri had threatened to do, prepared for a fight to the death. In the end, the army negotiated a peaceful stand-down. But before that happened, an LDS militia slaughtered a wagon train of civilian settlers passing through LDS-held territory. This atrocity, the Mountain Meadows Massacre, inflamed public sentiment against Mormonism.

Back east, Mormons who had not followed Young established new communities of their own in places including Iowa, Texas, and Pennsylvania. At first, the largest of these rival Mormon movements was led by James Strang, whose followers gathered to communities in Wisconsin and Michigan. But in a familiar pattern, the Strangite communities soon struggled with internal dissension and external opposition. By the mid-1850s, Strang was trying to rule as a polygamous king. Alienated followers shot him, and his movement collapsed.

Many Strangites then shifted their allegiance to yet another Mormon movement that was coming into being at this time. This new movement was the work of Mormons who had scattered through the Midwest following Joseph Smith Jr.'s death. After several years, these Mormons decided that God was inspiring them to form the *Reorganized* Church of Jesus Christ of Latter Day Saints, known more simply as the Reorganization or RLDS Church. They asked

Smith's oldest son, Joseph Smith III, to head the organization as prophet-president; in 1860, he accepted. The second largest Mormon denomination after the LDS Church, the Reorganization set about charting a different kind of Mormonism than that practiced by the LDS farther west.

The first thirty years of Mormon history were highly eventful and tumultuous. Mormons built and abandoned multiple settlements, including Independence, the movement's sacred center place. Mormons and non-Mormons clashed violently, and the Mormon movement split into different streams with diverging visions for what Mormonism should be. Although the LDS stream fled U.S. territory following Joseph Smith Jr.'s death, the westward expansion of the United States left them with nowhere else to run. By 1860, it was clear that both the LDS and the Reorganization needed to negotiate a peaceful coexistence with other Americans.

MORMONISM AND BLACK AFRICANS

White racism has shaped the history of every American Christian group. But racist policies persisted unusually long in some streams of Mormonism partly due to teachings written into Mormonism's unique scriptures. The Book of Mormon states that God caused "a skin of blackness" to come upon a people called Lamanites, supposed to be ancestors of today's Native Americans, as a curse for their having rejected God's commands.[1] Joseph Smith Jr. similarly taught that "a blackness" had come upon another ancient people, the people of Canaan, perhaps intended as a reference to descendants of Cain.[2] Yet another text produced by Smith, the Book of Abraham, states that Noah's son Ham married a Canaanite woman and that their descendants "could not have the right of Priesthood."[3]

Among the LDS, these texts lent support to a policy, implemented under Brigham Young, that barred people of black African ancestry from being ordained to the priesthood or participating in temple rites (which bestowed blessings connected to the priesthood). The ordination ban meant that black males could not serve in church leadership or bless and baptize their family members as other LDS males could do. The temple ban meant that black individuals could not receive rites, including eternal marriage, that LDS believed were necessary to attain the highest level of salvation. These policies in turn discouraged LDS members of other races from marrying black individuals. These restrictions did not apply, however, to people whom LDS understood as descended from Lamanites – including Native Americans and Pacific Islanders – perhaps because the Book of Mormon promised that if Lamanites returned to God's ways, they would become "white" (later revised to say "pure").

As a result of the new black priesthood ban, an African American named Elijah Abel, who had been ordained during Joseph Smith Jr.'s lifetime, was no longer allowed to officiate in most priesthood roles. Another African American, Jane Manning James, repeatedly petitioned LDS leaders to let her receive temple rites that she claimed Smith had promised her.

The Reorganization did not implement a black priesthood ban. (Since the Reorganization didn't practice temple rites, there was never any question of a black temple ban.) At the end of the Civil War, as RLDS leaders contemplated launching missions among newly freed African Americans, Joseph Smith III produced a revelation in which God commanded the RLDS to "ordain Priests unto me, of every race."[4] Lacking a black priesthood ban, the Reorganization was able to start building congregations in parts of the world, such as Haiti and Africa, where the LDS didn't send missionaries since they wouldn't have been able to ordain local leaders. In 2000, a Zambian named Bunda Chibwe was appointed to the RLDS Church's Council of Twelve Apostles, the first black individual to fill so high an office in any Mormon denomination.

The LDS priesthood ban received little criticism in the United States until the rise of the black civil rights movement in the 1950s–1960s. Then the ban attracted considerable controversy. Elsewhere in the world, the ban created difficulties as seemingly white LDS converts in places like Brazil and South Africa were unable to prove they had no black ancestry, or discovered they had black ancestry *after* being ordained or receiving temple rites. In the 1960s–1970s, LDS leaders found themselves in an awkward position after being contacted by Ghanaians and Nigerians who had encountered LDS literature and organized themselves into congregations, apparently unaware of the black priesthood ban.

In 1978, LDS church president Spencer W. Kimball announced that he had received a revelation rescinding the priesthood ban. Blacks could now participate in the church on equal terms with everyone else. Since then, the LDS Church has grown, and built temples, in Africa and in places with African diaspora populations, such as Brazil and the Caribbean. As of 2015, two black men – one Brazilian, one Kenyan – have served among the Seventy, the lower tiers of the church's global leadership councils.

LDS leaders have never stated that the black priesthood ban was wrong. They have said that the church "disavows the theories advanced in the past that black skin is a sign of divine disfavor or curse."[5] But this statement does not disavow the ban, only the theological justifications that the LDS had used for the ban. It appears that church leaders continue to regard the ban as divinely revealed, for reasons known only to God, then divinely rescinded.

Meanwhile, Fundamentalists still hold to nineteenth-century LDS teachings that supported the black priesthood ban. But Fundamentalists usually attract criticism for reasons other than their views on race – namely, polygamy and abuses associated with it.

1860–1920: PATHWAYS TO AMERICANIZATION

During their movement's first three decades, Mormons were accused of being un-American. In a Protestant-dominated society, Mormons weren't orthodox Protestants; their prophet-led communities were regarded as undemocratic; their theocratic ideas were inconsistent with church–state separation. However, the decades between the Civil War and World War I transformed Mormons' relationships to American society. During this time, the LDS and the Reorganization adapted in different ways to the dominant American norms of the time. In other words, Mormons in different streams of the movement adopted different strategies for Americanization. This happened during a period in history when other American religious minorities – including Catholics, Native Americans, and Asians – likewise experienced pressure to Americanize. The Reorganization adapted more willingly than the LDS, who bent to the norms of the American majority only after a long struggle against the U.S. government.

The LDS had gone west in order to establish holy communities according to the pattern that Mormons had developed at Nauvoo. These communities would be theocratic, communitarian, and polygamous. Citing teachings that Joseph Smith Jr. had given secretly before his death, LDS leaders maintained that God had commanded Mormons to practice polygamy as a new dimension of the project of building holy communities. Family bonds were holy; the purpose of polygamy was to enlarge those holy bonds, creating ever-widening circles of family members united to one another and to God. About a quarter of the LDS lived in polygamous households, most frequently consisting of one husband and two wives.

As U.S. rule became better established in Utah following the Civil War, and as more non-Mormons moved into the territory, the LDS struggled to preserve their vision of a holy community. They tried to preserve theocratic principles by forming their own church-directed political party and turning to church leaders, not the federal courts, to resolve disputes. LDS boycotted non-Mormon businesses in favor of their own economic cooperatives, an effort to implement the law of consecration. LDS leaders tried to offset the growth of the non-Mormon population by helping tens of thousands of converts, mostly British and Scandinavian, "gather to Zion" – that is, emigrate to Utah. LDS missionaries made converts during this period in Mexico and the Pacific islands as well. However, these non-white converts, unlike European converts, were not typically gathered to the American west; they stayed where they were. White racism was a factor in this discrepancy, but the presence of non-white LDS in Mexico and the Pacific had the effect of expanding Mormonism outside the United States.

Although the conflicts were no longer bloody, as they had been during the 1830s–1850s, the LDS continued to face vigorous opposition from outsiders throughout the latter half of the 1800s. Flush with their success at abolishing slavery, Protestant reformers were determined to further improve their nation: by eliminating the evils of alcohol, by "civilizing" Native Americans, and by ending Mormon polygamy. Between the 1860s and the 1880s, Congress passed a series of laws expanding the government's power to prosecute polygamists, a campaign that the LDS dubbed "the Raid." Eventually LDS citizens were stripped of their right to vote, and Congress declared the LDS Church legally dissolved. After arguing unsuccessfully before the Supreme Court that the Constitution's guarantees of free religious exercise should protect their practice of polygamy, the LDS capitulated. Beginning in 1890, church leaders declared that the LDS should submit to the law of the land: God had revealed to them that they should suspend the practice of polygamy so that the church could continue its work of missionizing the world and administering the rites necessary for salvation. (See chapters 3 and 4 for fuller discussions of church–state struggles around Mormonism and the practice of polygamy.)

The end of polygamy was one facet of a larger process of change as the LDS, crossing into the twentieth century, adapted to dominant American norms. The LDS dismantled their theocratic institutions: their political party, their economic cooperatives, and their separate church courts. Attempts to practice the law of consecration disappeared. During the Raid, LDS leaders had anticipated God's final judgment on the world at any moment; now those expectations became vaguer as the LDS began to participate fully in American society. With the end of polygamy, Congress finally granted Utah statehood, and the LDS quickly moved into national politics, using their numbers and economic influence in the west to their advantage. The literal "gathering to Zion" ended as LDS leaders urged converts outside the United States not to emigrate but to build up the church where they were, a policy change that led to growing LDS communities in Europe. The LDS movement in the early twentieth century looked less like a kingdom and more like American Protestants' conception of a church: one religious denomination among many.

The Reorganization was much less resistant to dominant American norms than the LDS and therefore escaped the opposition that the LDS faced. During the latter 1800s, as the LDS struggled to preserve polygamy, the Reorganization developed an alternative vision of how to be Mormon, one that could fit more easily into Protestant-dominated American society. The Reorganization rejected many developments in Mormon teaching and practice that had been introduced in Nauvoo – polygamy and theocracy among them – insisting that these had originated with Brigham Young, not Joseph Smith Jr. The Reorganization built on an earlier version of Mormonism, one that differed less dramatically from conventional Protestantism than the LDS version. The Reorganization embraced the Book of Mormon and other revelations from Joseph Smith Jr. as scripture, and they retained much of the church structure and many of the rites that Smith had introduced into Mormonism during the 1830s, before Nauvoo. But because they did not aspire to create theocratic communities or practice polygamy, the Reorganization avoided conflict with the U.S. government. Also, the Reorganization placed less emphasis on adherents literally gathering together, which meant that they lived more "in the world" than the LDS had hoped to do.

During the controversy around polygamy, the Reorganization was eager to distance itself from the LDS and to assert itself as the true expression of Mormon teaching. The fact that the Reorganization was led by Joseph Smith Jr.'s son was a point of pride and, indeed, an article of faith: until the late twentieth century, the Reorganization held that the church should always be led by one of the founder's direct descendants – none of whom had gone west with the LDS. The Reorganization was also proud to own the first Mormon temple, built in Kirtland, Ohio, in the 1830s. In 1920, the Reorganization took another step to associate itself with a potent Mormon sacred site by moving its headquarters to Independence, Missouri. While the LDS in Utah talked of someday returning to their Zion in Missouri, the Reorganization had done it. Thousands of Reorganization members lived in Independence, worshipping in dozens of congregations, while only a handful of LDS lived in the area. Furthermore, the Reorganization competed with the LDS for the allegiance of Mormons living outside the United States. Benefiting from the chaos created in the LDS Church by the long anti-polygamy campaign, missionaries for the Reorganization won the allegiance of 2,000 Mormon converts made in French Polynesia before Joseph Smith

Jr.'s death; that nation would remain an important hub in the Reorganization's global presence.

At the beginning of the 1910s, both the LDS Church and the Reorganization were led by relatives of Joseph Smith Jr. The Reorganization was led by his son, Joseph Smith III; the LDS Church was led by the founder's nephew, Joseph F. Smith. Joseph Smith III died in 1914; Joseph F. Smith, in 1918. Their deaths symbolized the passing of generations personally linked to the Mormon founder and thus mark the end of a formative era in Mormon history. By the time of the Smiths' deaths, both the LDS Church and the Reorganization had, in different ways, adapted to American norms while still asserting distinctive religious identities. As the twentieth century brought new social changes, Mormonism's diverging streams would undergo further changes as well.

1910–1960: MODERNIZERS AND FUNDAMENTALISTS

In 1911, nearly the entire 114-member student body at Brigham Young University, a fledgling LDS school in Utah, rallied to the defense of three professors who had come under censure from church officials for teaching biological evolution and modern biblical criticism. Despite the overwhelming support of their students, the professors were forced to resign. The incident symbolizes two important developments in Mormon history in the early twentieth century. First, the very existence of Brigham Young University is a sign that Mormons, having set themselves on the path of Americanization, aspired in the early twentieth century to build the kinds of institutions, such as colleges, that longer-established churches had created. Second, the controversy around evolution and biblical criticism represents a new kind of internal struggle among Mormons over what their movement should look like in the twentieth century: a struggle between those who embraced changes associated with modern times and those who defended older traditions.

By the beginning of the twentieth century, forces of modernization had transformed American society. Massive urbanization had occurred, driven partly by huge waves of immigration; the resulting concentration of cheap labor facilitated the rise of modern industry. Immigration also resulted in dramatic growth for non-Protestant religious groups in the United States, which led in turn to former "outsiders" now pushing back against the idea that being truly American meant being Protestant. The growing Catholic and Jewish populations were determined to be recognized as American, too — and by the 1950s, they had secured that recognition in the dominant view. This shift in American society was beneficial to Mormons as well. All through the 1800s, opposition to Mormonism had come chiefly from Protestants who saw Mormonism as incompatible with a Protestant nation. In the early twentieth century the idea of America as a Protestant nation gave way to notions of a Judeo-Christian nation, a category broad enough to include Mormons. Mormons at the middle of the twentieth century fit more comfortably in American society than at any time before or since.

The change was particularly dramatic for the LDS, coming as it did after decades of opposition. The LDS became a respected, if marginal, American church. American LDS fought for their country in both world wars. In the 1950s, a future LDS church president, Ezra Taft Benson, served on U.S. president Dwight Eisenhower's cabinet. Family life was another area where the LDS became more like other Americans. LDS leaders continued to teach, as they had in the polygamy era, that marriage and family linked people in holy bonds to God and one another; but now the family type being celebrated was the monogamous nuclear family. Commitment to this conventional kind of family life became a central and well-known feature of LDS identity.

During the first half of the twentieth century both the LDS and the Reorganization invested in creating modern institutions that could provide cradle-to-grave support for their members. These institutions afforded Mormons the solid respectability of other denominations; at the same time, they represented modern approaches to building up and sustaining holy communities. The Reorganization and the LDS were the very first churches to start Boy Scouting programs west of the Mississippi, and both groups started youth and young adult programs inspired by similar programs among Protestants. Mormons established hospitals and nursing homes, church bureaucracies and magazines. Both the LDS Church and the Reorganization erected new church buildings in city after city during the 1950s, part of a larger boom in the construction of churches and synagogues in the United States. In addition, the Reorganization began construction on an outsized new headquarters facility in Independence in

1925, complete with a conference hall and organ to rival the already famous Salt Lake Tabernacle, which the LDS had built during the 1800s. Institutions like these announced that Mormonism was a modern, growing movement.

But efforts to be modern occasioned new internal conflicts within Mormonism's streams – conflicts between modernizers and traditionalists. Such conflicts affected other American religious groups of the time as well, most notably American Protestants, who by the 1920s had become deeply divided in what is known as the modernist-fundamentalist controversy. Modernists urged Protestants to adjust their views on scripture to the emerging fields of biblical studies and evolutionary biology. Also, modernists championed a "social gospel" that called Christians to dedicate themselves to social causes such as alleviating the exploitation of workers or the plight of people living in slums. Fundamentalists, on the other hand, perceived modernists as threatening the authority of scripture – throwing out Christianity's fundamental teachings for the sake of being intellectually fashionable. Fundamentalists condemned evolution and modern biblical criticism, and they suspected the social gospel of distracting vital attention from personal sin and personal salvation.

Modernist ideas entered both the LDS Church and the Reorganization during the period between the world wars, when members of those Mormon movements attended the University of Chicago Divinity School, a modernist center. LDS and RLDS modernists encouraged members of their movements to rethink aspects of Mormon belief that clashed with modern science – such as accepting that the Book of Mormon was a nineteenth-century composition, not an authentic ancient record – or to embrace liberal social causes in the name of Mormon values. Modernist ideas proved more influential in the Reorganization than in the LDS Church, where traditionalist church leaders moved to purge modernism from the church's publications and religious education programs. A trend was beginning to emerge that would become more pronounced later in the twentieth century: the Reorganization was more open to liberal trends in theology than the LDS.

Nevertheless, modernist thinking about the importance of social welfare found echoes among the LDS. During the Great Depression, LDS church leaders created a massive church welfare system, complete with ranches, farms, canning facilities, and distribution centers. The intent was to keep LDS members off the federal dole; thus the LDS welfare system can be understood both as a kind of Mormon social gospel and as hearkening back to the law of consecration, the early Mormon vision of a communitarian society independent from the outside world. During the same period, the Reorganization launched communitarian experiments in the form of small-scale collective farming. The Reorganization never developed a welfare system as complex as the LDS Church's; on the other hand, the Reorganization embraced the language of the social gospel more fully than the LDS. Reorganization members wrote tracts about how "Zionic principles" would solve labor problems, they authored novels about social reform that doubled as missionary tracts, and they advocated building exper-imental communities where labor and ownership would be shared in common. This was nineteenth-century Mormon communitarianism recast in the image of twentieth-century theological liberalism.

Just as modernism produced a fundamentalist backlash among Protestants, so too Mormon modernism led to the rise of new move-ments determined to preserve older ways. During the 1920s, several thousand members of the Reorganization revolted against moderniza-tion in their church. These members left the RLDS Church to join what until then had been a tiny Mormon sect called the Church of Christ (Temple Lot), so called because it claimed to own the plot of land that Joseph Smith Jr. had designated for building a temple in Independence. In subsequent decades, these alienated RLDS split several more times, over disputes caused by some members' claims to have received further revelations. All these groups have maintained an enduring, if tiny, presence in Independence, Mormonism's center place. (See chapter 6.)

A more significant traditionalist revolt occurred among the LDS, producing the third stream of Mormonism on which we focus in this book: the Fundamentalists. The modern innovation centrally opposed by Fundamentalists was the LDS Church's abandonment of polygamy. A Fundamentalist network coalesced in the 1920s around Loren C. Woolley, who taught that God's command to practice polygamy remained in force and that he held divine authority to per-form plural marriages. Fundamentalist families gathered to a remote region on the Utah-Arizona border known as Short Creek, where they hoped to practice polygamy undisturbed. Fundamentalist groups proliferated as the twentieth century progressed, some produced by splits within Woolley's movement, others formed by yet more groups of dissatisfied LDS longing for the Mormonism of Brigham Young's day. Consequently, there are now several different Fundamentalist groups, with communities in various rural locations in western North America. The largest groups are the Fundamentalist Church of Jesus Christ of Latter-Day Saints (FLDS) and the Apostolic United Brethren (AUB), both descended from Woolley's movement, each with several thousand members. Other Fundamentalists, called "independents," practice polygamy without belonging to an organized group. In addition to polygamy, Fundamentalist communities often aspire to practice the law of consecration through some form of economic communitarianism. Meanwhile, the now-monogamous LDS denounced Fundamentalists and objected strenuously on occasions when the media referred to Fundamentalists as "Mormons." Since Fundamentalists were not in harmony with the LDS Church, the LDS argued, they were not truly Mormon.

The reemergence of Mormon polygamy in Fundamentalist communities generated a legal backlash in the mid-twentieth century as it had in the 1800s. In 1953, law enforcement officials from Arizona descended on the Fundamentalist community at Short Creek, arresting many of the men and taking their children into state custody. However, between the anti-polygamy Raid of the 1800s and the Short Creek Raid of the 1950s, something had changed in American society. Media coverage of the Short Creek Raid was largely sympathetic to the polygamists, whom journalists portrayed as victims of overreaching state government. The Fundamentalists fared better than LDS polygamists of the 1800s: after the negative publicity, the government returned the community's children and left the polygamists alone. Meanwhile, the raid gave Fundamentalists the sense of being a persecuted people, like their polygamous forebearers of the 1800s – thus bolstering their conviction that they were the true Mormons.

By the mid-1950s, then, Mormonism had developed three major streams: the LDS, the Reorganization, and the Fundamentalists. If we arrange these three groups along a spectrum from theologically liberal to conservative, the Reorganization would be left-leaning, the LDS would be right-leaning, and the Fundamentalists would be radical-right. Yet all three major divisions of Mormonism enjoyed a relatively positive relationship with American society at large. The Reorganization was little known outside of the midwestern United

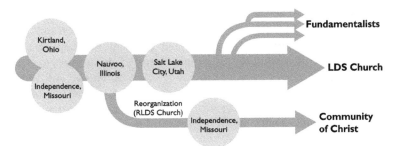

Figure 1.1 The historical development of the three Mormon streams. The locations that appear on the graphic are the changing headquarters of early Mormonism and its diverging streams.

Image courtesy of John Hamer.

States, but they were well accepted by their neighbors there. LDS had gained acceptance as moral, hard-working, family-oriented, patriotic citizens. Even polygamous Fundamentalists, remarkably, had become a symbol of citizens' right to live free of undue government interference.

The story of Mormon modernization and its discontents during the first half of the twentieth century is a story about *American* Mormons because the membership of all the Mormon movements was still predominantly American. Nevertheless, as American foreign power increased after World War I, so did the Mormon presence abroad. The LDS expanded their missionary presence to South America, Asia, and eastern Europe, while the Reorganization, on a smaller scale, extended its missions in Europe, Australia, and French Polynesia. By 1947, there were one million LDS worldwide, while the Reorganization numbered about 150,000: both movements had doubled in size in forty years. During the second half of the twentieth century, these movements would build themselves up internationally on a still greater scale. In the process, they would face new conflicts and undergo new changes.

1945–PRESENT: GLOBAL EXPANSION

In the aftermath of World War II, the world changed dramatically. The empires that Western nations had built during the 1800s broke up as colonies in Africa and Asia gained independence. In this new postcolonial world, two superpowers, the United States and the Soviet Union, competed to spread their ideologies and spheres of influence. By the end of the twentieth century, Communist governments in the Soviet Union and its European satellites had collapsed, leaving the United States dominant in a new economic order dubbed globalization. American culture was exported worldwide: Coca-Cola, McDonalds, MTV, Hollywood – and religion. American missionaries worked around the world, benefiting from the privileged access to other countries afforded to American travelers. American religious organizations used rapidly advancing communication technologies to take their messages global – for instance, through televangelism. At the same time, non-Western peoples were more assertive about the value of their own cultures, even as they absorbed, borrowed, and adapted American culture for their own circumstances and interests.

Mormonism joined other American religions in going global. This was not true of the Fundamentalists, who lacked the resources for missionary efforts; some lacked even the inclination, content to see themselves as a small faithful remnant in a world ripe for destruction. But the LDS and the Reorganization greatly expanded their missions outside of North America. In the process, these two movements developed diverging strategies for creating holy communities that crossed cultural boundaries.

As a result of the American baby boom, which followed World War II, by the 1960s there was a huge cohort of LDS young people available to serve as missionaries. The church harnessed that potential by urging every young man to donate eighteen months to two years of his time to serve a mission. By the outset of the twenty-first century, LDS missionaries were working by the tens of thousands around the globe. Most were young men, serving in what had become a standard uniform of white shirts, ties, and black name badges; but young women and retired couples served as well. As the numbers of missionaries grew, so did LDS growth outside the United States – dramatically. In 1960, the LDS claimed over 1.5 million members; by 2015, the figure was 15 million. In 1960, 90% of LDS were American; by the 1990s, only 50% were American. By far, most LDS growth outside the United States was in Latin America: by the early twenty-first century, nearly half of the LDS worldwide were Spanish-speaking.

Although it lagged far behind the LDS Church's millions of converts, the Reorganization also grew rapidly outside of the United States during the 1960s and 1970s, adding tens of thousands of members in only twenty years. The Reorganization's greatest growth occurred in Haiti, India, and certain African nations, notably Nigeria and the Democratic Republic of the Congo. One in four of the Reorganization's members were French-speaking by the beginning of the twenty-first century. Many of the places where the Reorganization flourished – Haiti and Africa – were places where LDS missionaries didn't work until after 1978 as a result of the LDS Church's black priesthood ban. (See the essay that accompanies this chapter, "Mormonism and Black Africans.")

Rapid international growth, at a period in history when respect for cultural diversity was a dominant social value, required both LDS and Reorganization leaders to reconsider the relationship between Mormonism and American culture. How much of what American Mormons were accustomed to doing needed to be replicated in other parts of the world in order for the communities there to be authentically Mormon? Which beliefs and customs were truly essential – that is, universally applicable revelations from God? Which reflected an American cultural setting and could therefore be modified elsewhere?

As we will discuss at greater length in chapter 7, the LDS and the Reorganization responded to these questions with different strategies. The LDS strategy, known as "correlation," sought to winnow Mormonism down to basic principles that could be applied in all cultural settings. In theory, LDS in different parts of the world would be free to develop different ways of applying those basic principles, appropriate to their local circumstances. In practice, however, correlation had the effect of promoting uniformity by encouraging worldwide conformity to an institutional culture that LDS leaders insisted was not distinctively American although it originated at the church's American headquarters in Salt Lake City. Perceptions that the LDS Church was an American institution proved lethal at times – as in parts of Latin America during the 1980s and 1990s, when LDS meetinghouses were bombed and missionaries killed by leftist militants.

The Reorganization took a different approach to cultural diversity. RLDS leaders, influenced by trends in Catholic and Protestant thinking about missions in the late twentieth century, advocated a process of "indigenization" that would let the gospel take different forms in different cultural settings, and it promoted forms of church governance that would allow greater autonomy to members in different parts of the world. As a result, Reorganization congregations in other parts of the world only vaguely resembled congregations in the American Midwest. For instance, in Haiti and India, the areas of the Reorganization's greatest growth, converts decided that the Book of Mormon wasn't relevant to them, and they therefore used only the Bible as scripture – a development that would have been unthinkable for the LDS. In the 2010s, the Reorganization's internal diversity resulted in a situation where the church performed same-sex marriages in some countries but not in others – again, unthinkable for the LDS. By contrast to the more strongly homogenous worldwide identity of the LDS, the Reorganization had become an international patchwork of diverse groups, struggling to decide what it meant to call themselves one church.

The dramatic surges in Mormon membership after the 1960s did not continue indefinitely. The Reorganization's growth leveled off beginning in the 1980s, while LDS growth showed signs of leveling or dipping in the early twenty-first century. In 2015, the LDS reported 15 million members, but some observers estimated that less than a third of that number still participated in the church; many may have switched to other faiths. The Reorganization's main denomination had 200,000 members worldwide. Estimates of the Fundamentalists' numbers varied, but a ballpark figure is 40,000, nearly all living in the United States. Meanwhile, in Mormonism's American center, late twentieth-century social changes were generating new internal conflicts and new opposition from outsiders.

1960–PRESENT: A CHANGING AMERICAN RELIGIOUS LANDSCAPE

In May 1970, the only RLDS to have served as a U.S. senator, Milton Young of North Dakota, gave the commencement address at Graceland College, the Reorganization's small liberal arts school in Lamoni, Iowa. Young was a conservative Republican who had voted against civil rights legislation and supported widening the war in Vietnam. As Young shook hands with the college graduates, one young man, a budding peace activist, slipped the senator a note imploring him, in words echoing one of Joseph Smith Jr.'s revelations, to "renounce war and proclaim peace."

This anecdote captures a dramatic shift that occurred on the American religious landscape in the wake of the social and cultural upheavals of the 1960s. For much of American history, the major religious divides had been between different religious traditions: Protestants and Catholics, Christians and Jews. After the 1960s, Americans became religiously polarized in a different way: along a conservative-liberal divide that cut across religious traditions. Members of the same religious tradition, like Milton Young and the student peace activist, found themselves divided by new controversies: civil rights, U.S. foreign policy, issues of gender and sexuality. As members of religious traditions became divided from one another over these issues, conservatives in one religious tradition found they had more in common with conservatives in other religious traditions than with liberals in their own tradition, and vice versa for liberals. Mormons in the United States experienced this same dynamic. In the process, Mormons developed new affinities with people in other religious traditions but also attracted new opponents.

The post-1960s conservative-liberal divide within Mormonism was most intense in controversies around women's roles and homosexuality. Although LDS and RLDS were divided *within* their churches over these issues, on the whole the LDS leaned conservative while the RLDS leaned liberal. In the 1980s, the Reorganization followed the lead of several other Christian or Jewish denominations and began to ordain women. This change alienated about one-fourth of the Reorganization's members in the United States, who dropped out to form small rival groups known as Restorationists. Meanwhile, although a minority of LDS members advocated women's ordination, the majority followed LDS leaders in rejecting it, maintaining that men and women had different divinely ordained roles to play. Controversies around homosexuality likewise created division within each church, but on the whole the LDS remained more conservative while the Reorganization moved in a more liberal direction. LDS leadership maintained that sexual expression should be confined to the marriage of a man and a woman, while RLDS in the United States voted in the 2010s to authorize same-sex marriages. (We'll discuss these controversies in more detail in chapter 4.)

Another important shift on the post-1960s American religious landscape was an expansion of religious pluralism. As new religious movements attracted followings among the Baby Boomers – Asian religions, for example – there developed a wider sense among Americans that religious diversity should be affirmatively valued. This was an important shift from the 1800s, when religious minorities such as Mormons had faced suspicion or legal restrictions from the Protestant majority. At the same time, however, two new developments pulled against the trend towards religious pluralism. One was a late twentieth-century surge in the growth of American Protestantism's theologically conservative wing, often called evangelicalism. Evangelicals maintained that Christianity – more specifically, their conservative form of it – was the only path to salvation, and many spoke of a need to preserve America's Christian (or Judeo-Christian) values. The second trend pulling against pluralism was the emergence of an "anti-cult movement," formed of people who were alarmed by the growth of new religions that they believed were coercive or harmed their members.

The rise of evangelicalism and the anti-cult movement generated a new wave of opposition to Mormonism in the final decades of the twentieth-century, focused especially on the LDS Church, by far the largest and most visible Mormon movement. Evangelicals, much like Protestants in the nineteenth century, criticized Mormonism as a false religion – a "cult." Evangelicals regarded the LDS as major rivals in missionizing, in part because in key respects they were alike: both believed they taught the one true path to salvation through Christ; both were conservative in how they interpreted their scriptures and in their moral values. LDS were particularly offended by evangelicals' insistence that Mormonism was not authentically Christian. Persuading the public that their religion was Christian became a major preoccupation of the LDS at the end of the twentieth century; this had not been the case earlier in the century, before the evangelical resurgence. (See chapter 2 for more on the "Are Mormons Christian?" question.)

Where the LDS had affinities – and therefore rivalry – with conservative Protestants, the Reorganization developed stronger ties with more liberal kinds of Protestants. Starting in the 1960s, RLDS leaders and theologians moved away from understanding Mormonism as the uniquely authorized restoration of Christ's true church and toward seeing themselves as one Christian tradition among many. These RLDS leaders emphasized the Bible much more than distinctively Mormon scriptures such as the Book of Mormon. This emerging brand of liberal Mormon theology held that the mission of the Reorganization was not to convert the world to the one true church, but to promote values of peace, hope, joy, and love in the world. Two concrete changes symbolized this shift in the Reorganization's identity. First, the Reorganization stopped requiring that its prophet-president be a descendant of Joseph Smith Jr., as had been the case since 1860. Second, the organization changed its name from "Reorganized Church of Jesus Christ of Latter Day Saints" to "Community of Christ."

Starting in the late 1970s, some evangelicals and other religious conservatives organized themselves politically to defend what they regarded as traditional American values, launching campaigns against abortion, pornography, same-sex marriage, and secularism. This political movement was known as the religious right. The conservative-leaning LDS made natural allies for the religious right. This was especially true on issues involving families, which played a special role in LDS teachings about holy living; in the post-1960s period, those teachings translated into an LDS commitment to "traditional family values." With their nationwide membership and considerable financial resources, the LDS became key supporters of some religious right campaigns — most famously, the effort to block a constitutional amendment on gender equality in the 1970s–1980s, which opponents feared would undermine traditional gender roles, and a campaign to keep same-sex marriage illegal in California in 2008. However, relations between the LDS and the religious right were complicated by the fact that conservative evangelicals, the dominant group in the religious right, were leery about collaborating with the LDS because of their theological objections to the Mormon "cult." These tensions were evident when LDS Mitt Romney, running for U.S. president in 2008 and 2012, had to navigate opposition from evangelicals within his own party.

But the Mormons who faced the most intense opposition at the beginning of the twenty-first century were the Fundamentalists. The anti-cult movement helped rally new public opposition to polygamous groups, whom anti-cult activists accused of sexually abusing young women, swindling members, and possibly posing a violent threat to their neighbors. FLDS church president Warren Jeffs was imprisoned for sex with underage girls whom he had taken as plural wives. In 2008, an FLDS settlement in Texas was raided by armed troopers acting on exaggerated information provided to them by anti-cult activists, an echo of the Short Creek Raid of 1953. At the same time, despite these difficulties, Fundamentalists benefited from the pluralistic climate of the post-1960s period. In this era, many Americans were inclined to be tolerant of religious and sexual minorities. Polygamous Mormon families, therefore, became the subject of sympathetic TV dramas and reality programs during the 2000s and 2010s.

As the religious landscape in the United States changed after the 1960s, all three of the Mormon movements we have been following adjusted to the new reality. The LDS oriented themselves toward the religious right and made a concerted effort to emphasize that their movement was Christian, not a "cult." The Reorganization very literally rebranded itself by changing its name to Community of Christ, symbolic of a theologically liberal shift in that movement. Fundamentalists continued to defend their constitutional right to practice polygamy and used the medium of television to present themselves as champions of American values: love of family and the right to choose your own way of life, even an unconventional one.

CONCLUSION

Within its first thirty years, Mormonism split into two major streams, the LDS and the Reorganization; within the movement's first hundred years, a third important stream, the Fundamentalists, had emerged as well. In less than two hundred years, Mormons' place in American society and on the larger world stage underwent dramatic shifts. In the early nineteenth century, Mormons experienced violent opposition. In the late nineteenth century crossing into the twentieth, most Mormons more-or-less willingly bent to the norms of American Protestant society – less willingly for the LDS than for the Reorganization. By the mid-twentieth century, Mormons in all three streams enjoyed a comfortable-to-tolerable position in American society – even the Fundamentalists, once the government had decided to look the other way. In the late twentieth century, the LDS and Reorganization expanded their international presence dramatically (although less dramatically than the LDS intimated). At the same time, Mormons in all three streams repositioned themselves within an American cultural landscape that had become more religiously pluralistic yet was anxious about "cults" and riven by a conservative-liberal divide.

At every stage in their movement's historical development, Mormons disagreed with one another over what their movement should teach, how their communities should be organized, in what ways they should either accommodate or resist trends in the society around them, and how they should present themselves to the larger world. In short, Mormons disagreed at every stage of their history over the question: what does it mean to be Mormon?

NOTES

1 2 Nephi 5:19–23 (LDS editions); II Nephi 4:29–38 (RLDS/Community of Christ editions).
2 Moses 7:8 (in the LDS Pearl of Great Price). The same text is found in Doctrine and Covenants 36:1i (RLDS/Community of Christ editions).
3 Abraham 1:21–27 (in the LDS Pearl of Great Price).
4 Doctrine and Covenants 116 (RLDS/Community of Christ editions).
5 "Race and the Priesthood," undated statement published online in December 2013, available at lds.org.

SUGGESTIONS FOR FURTHER READING

Matthew Bowman, *The Mormon People: The Making of an American Faith* (New York: Random House, 2012).

Newell C. Bringhurst and John C. Hamer, eds., *Scattering of the Saints: Schism within Mormonism* (Independence, MO: John Whitmer Books, 2007).

Terryl L. Givens and Philip L. Barlow, eds., *The Oxford Handbook of Mormonism* (New York: Oxford University Press, 2015).

Cardell K. Jacobson and Lara Burton, eds., *Modern Polygamy in the United States: Historical, Cultural, and Legal Issues* (New York: Oxford University Press, 2011).

Armand L. Mauss, *All Abraham's Children: Changing Mormon Conceptions of Race and Lineage* (Urbana: University of Illinois Press, 2003).

Mark A. Scherer, *The Journey of a People: The Era of the Reorganization, 1844–1946* (Independence, MO: Community of Christ Seminary Press, 2013).

2

ARE MORMONS CHRISTIAN? WHY DOES IT MATTER?

MORMONISM AND RELIGIOUS PLURALISM

In February 2007, former Massachusetts governor Mitt Romney held a town hall meeting in Florida as part of his first campaign to run for U.S. president. One man attending the meeting announced that he intended to vote for a candidate "who stands for the Lord Jesus Christ – and you, sir, you're a pretender. You do not know the Lord. You're a Mormon." Other people in the audience gasped, groaned, or booed. Romney responded with a calm chuckle. "Let me offer just a thought," he said. "One of the great things about this great land is we have people of different faiths and different persuasions. And I'm convinced that the nation does need to have people of different faiths, but we need to have a person *of faith* lead the country." The audience came to their feet in applause.

The claim that Romney, because he was Mormon, was not a Christian dogged him for the rest of his first campaign. It might seem odd that it would matter whether or not an American presidential candidate is Christian, given the United States' tradition of religious freedom and church–state separation. But to some American voters, it did matter. They wanted a Christian for president, and they did not believe that Romney qualified. The more Romney protested that Mormonism *is* a Christian religion, the more vehemently some American Christians – including prominent political figures – insisted that it is not. Four years later, Romney did win the

Republican nomination for president (losing to Barack Obama). But on the way, Romney had to reconcile himself to being unable to persuade a significant segment of his own party's voter base that he was, in fact, Christian.

Like other religious minorities in the United States, Mormons have had to come to terms with living in a country that promises religious freedom yet has been dominated by certain Christian groups. In the past, dominant Christians have pushed Mormons and other religious minorities to the margins of American culture; at times, dominant Christians have even threatened Mormons and other religious minorities with violence. The situation has changed as Americans have become more supportive of religious pluralism. Pluralism is an attitude that treats many different religions as worthy of celebration and equal respect; when Romney won applause for his remark about America needing people of different faiths, he was appealing to a pluralist vision of America. The emergence of a more pluralist environment has improved the situation of religious minorities. Nevertheless, the story of Mormonism's rocky relationship with American Christianity shows that even in the present, a religious minority's ability to win acceptance in American society can still be impacted by how closely their religion does or does not resemble certain kinds of Christianity.

In this chapter, you'll read about:

- A bigger picture: Christianity and religious pluralism in the United States.
- Why do people say Mormonism isn't Christian?
- Evolving theologies: the historical layers of Mormonism.
- The three streams of Mormonism and the American Christian mainstream.

A BIGGER PICTURE: CHRISTIANITY AND RELIGIOUS PLURALISM IN THE UNITED STATES

The kind of Christianity that has dominated U.S. society for most of the nation's history emerged in Europe not long after Columbus encountered the Americas. In the early 1500s, Christians in some parts of western Europe protested against financial corruption in the church, as well as against church teachings and traditions that they believed strayed from the Bible. When the Pope proved resistant to the reforms that the protesters wanted, the protesters rejected the Pope's authority and began forming churches of their own. Christians who remained loyal to the Pope came to be known as Catholics; the protesters who broke away were known as Protestants. The Protestants split into various groups, sometimes because of geography (different churches for different countries), other times because they disagreed about how to reform Christianity.

The vast majority of the Europeans who settled in the American colonies that eventually became the United States were Protestants of one kind or another. Perhaps you've heard of some of these groups: Anglicans (later known as Episcopalians), Reformed, Lutherans, Presbyterians, Baptists, Quakers, Methodists. Besides these various Protestant groups, the American colonies were also home to small Catholic minorities and even smaller communities of Jews. What's important to understand is this: when the newly born United States began creating laws to protect religious freedom, by far most of the groups on site to claim this freedom were Protestant, groups who despite their differences had quite a lot in common. In other words: at the beginning of U.S. history, religious tolerance was primarily a question of asking Protestants to tolerate other Protestants, plus a smattering of Catholics and Jews – a modest demand, compared to what would be asked of Americans over the course of the next century.

During the first half of the 1800s, the United States became more religiously diverse. The numbers of Catholics and Jews surged due to Irish and German immigration. The climate of religious freedom facilitated the growth of new kinds of Christian movements: Unitarians, liberal Christians who regarded Jesus as human, not divine; Universalists, who taught that God would leave no one in hell forever but would eventually bring everyone to heaven; Shakers, who practiced celibacy and believed that their founder was a female incarnation of God; Millerites, later called Adventists, who predicted the world would end on a certain date in 1844; and Mormons. During the second half of the 1800s, religious diversity in the United States expanded even further: still more Catholic immigrants, now from places like Italy and Poland; vast numbers of Jews from eastern Europe and Russia; Eastern Orthodox Christians from Greece and the Middle East;

Chinese Confucians and Taoists; Japanese Buddhists; Sikhs from the Punjab region of India. At the same time, some whites became attracted to the teachings of Hindu gurus. And still more new movements were born in the United States, including Jehovah's Witnesses, Christian Scientists, Theosophists, and at the start of the twentieth century, Pentecostals.

The expanding religious diversity alarmed many American Protestants. They especially feared the growth of Catholics, since in Protestants' minds, Catholicism equalled tyranny: a power-hungry religious hierarchy who told people what to think and who wanted to undermine freedom and democracy. As for new movements like Shakers, Millerites, or Mormons, mainstream Protestants regarded them as superstitious and irrational – undesirable qualities in a democracy where citizens vote on how the country should be run. Protestant writers during the 1800s waged media campaigns, via books and newspapers, denouncing what they saw as other religious groups' theological errors or the dangers these groups posed to American democracy. In some cases, Protestants' hostility toward Catholics erupted into violence: riots and church burnings. During the second half of the 1800s, Protestant anxiety about religious minorities intertwined with racism to give birth to an ideology that insisted that America had been born as, and needed to remain, a country dominated by white Anglo-Saxon Protestants and their values. Guided by this ideology, the U.S. government passed laws in the 1920s that greatly restricted immigration and ensured that future immigrants would come mostly from countries with white Protestant populations; these restrictions remained in effect until the 1960s.

But during the first half of the twentieth century, some white American Protestants were repulsed by bigotry against minorities, particularly against the nation's largest religious minorities: Catholics and Jews. Liberal-minded Protestants promoted a new ideology of America's religious identity: America was not a Protestant nation, but a "Judeo-Christian" one. By the 1950s, this broader way of understanding America's religious identity had become dominant. A sign of how much things had changed was the election, in 1960, of John F. Kennedy as the country's first Catholic president. Anti-Catholicism had gone out of fashion; so too had anti-Semitism.

Within just a couple of decades, though, the ideology of a Judeo-Christian America began to strike some Americans as still too narrow. The 1920s-era immigration restrictions were lifted in the 1960s, leading to increased numbers of Muslims, Buddhists, and Hindus moving into the United States. The 1960s also saw increased numbers of whites become interested in religions outside the Judeo-Christian mainstream: Buddhist meditation, Hindu yoga, Native American traditions, and New Age movements that talked about channeling, auras, or past lives. Another crop of brand-new religions appeared on the American scene, including Scientology, founded by sci-fi writer L. Ron Hubbard, and the Unification Church, known for its mass weddings. By the beginning of the twenty-first century, more and more Americans claimed no religious affiliation or identified themselves as "spiritual, not religious," picking and choosing their own personalized spiritualties.

In this post-1960s climate, some Americans challenged customs that implied a Judeo-Christian national identity. In a country as religiously diverse as the United States had become, was it appropriate for public schools to begin each day with a Bible reading and Judeo-Christian prayer? Was it appropriate to display the Ten Commandments, or Nativity scenes, in public schools and courthouses? Why should a Muslim legislator be expected to take his oath of office while holding his hand on a Bible? Religious minorities, supported by liberals in the Protestant mainstream, pressed the government to be more secular – that is, to remove Judeo-Christian symbols or practices from government spaces with the goal of creating a religiously neutral environment, one that didn't privilege some religions over others. That meant no teacher-led prayer and Bible reading in public schools; no Ten Commandments monuments in courthouses. In this way, secularism, the effort to keep American institutions religiously neutral, was wedded to pluralism, the effort to promote equality of religions in American society.

But these efforts produced a backlash, primarily from conservative Protestants, often referred to as evangelicals, joined by conservative-minded Catholics and Jews. Dubbed the religious right, these groups spoke of America's Judeo-Christian heritage as being under attack from secularists hostile to religion. At the end of the twentieth century and the beginning of the twenty-first, evangelicals were especially inclined to see themselves as having been reduced from the American mainstream, transmitters of the values on which the nation was founded, to a persecuted minority. Americans at the turn of the twenty-first century were arrayed along a spectrum of competing views, from expansive religious pluralism to conceptions of America as a Judeo-Christian, or simply Christian, nation. This struggle over how to define the nation's religious identity was the latest phase in a long history of tension between America's religious mainstream – Protestant, for most of the country's history – and various religious minorities.

Over the course of U.S. history, one way that religious minorities have responded to Protestant dominance is by adopting an image that makes them look somewhat more like Protestants, as a bid to appear more "normal" or mainstream. Most Jews living in the United States during the mid-1800s adopted reforms that made their houses of worship look more like churches: organs and choirs replaced chanting; a sermon became a key element of the service; families sat together in the pews, not segregated by sex. Various religious minorities in the United States, from Jews and Catholics to Muslims and Buddhists, adopted some variation of the nineteenth-century Protestant invention known as Sunday School. During World War II, Japanese-American Buddhists tried to make themselves seem less foreign by calling their congregations "churches" and their religious leaders "bishops" – terms that are Christian, not Buddhist. Early American Buddhists wrote Protestant-style hymns, quite different from traditional Buddhist chanting. American Catholics adopted many Protestant hymns as part of a massive liturgical reform during the 1960s; that same reform saw Catholics adopt some of the customs that Protestants and Catholics had fought about centuries earlier, such as worship in the language of the people (rather than in Latin). Growing support for pluralism has been an important factor in generating greater acceptance for religious minorities in the United States, but religious minorities' willingness to adapt to Protestant or Christian norms has also been a factor.

Having sketched this larger picture of the interplay between Protestant Christian dominance and religious pluralism over the course of U.S. history, now let's see how Mormons fit into the picture.

1600		
1700	The British American colonies are settled mostly by Protestants.	
1800	New movements: Unitarians, Universalists, Shakers, Adventists. Catholic immigration expands.	Mormonism begins.
	Protestants react hostilely to new groups. Anti-Catholic violence.	Anti-Mormon violence.
1850	New immigration: Catholics, Jews, Eastern Orthodox, Buddhists, Sikhs. New movements: Hindu devotees, Jehovah's Witnesses, Christian Scientists, Theosophists, Pentecostals.	RLDS embrace a more conventionally Christian form of Mormonism, avoid opposition.
	White Anglo-Saxon Protestants take steps to ensure that their values will dominate U.S. society.	Protestants press the government to end LDS polygamy.
1900		LDS retreat from polygamy and certain other distinctive teachings. Fundamentalists retain them.
1950	Liberal Protestants, Catholics, and Jews promote a "Judeo-Christian" America.	LDS and RLDS fit comfortably in the American mainstream. Short Creek Raid against Fundamentalists.
	New immigration: Muslims, Hindus, Buddhists. New movements: Scientology, Unification Church, New Age. Wider support for religious pluralism. Anxiety about "cults."	
	Ecumenical churches seek closer collaboration.	RLDS move closer toward ecumenical churches.
	Evangelicals and other religious conservatives oppose secularism, defend "Judeo-Christian" values.	Evangelical criticisms of LDS become more visible. LDS become more visibly Christ-centered, develop evangelical affinities.
2000		RLDS become Community of Christ, join National Council of Churches.
		Fundamentalists face anti-cult and government opposition. Raid at Yearning for Zion Ranch.

Figure 2.1 Parallel timeline relating developments in Mormonism to the broader history of religious pluralism in the United States.

WHY DO PEOPLE SAY MORMONISM ISN'T CHRISTIAN?

The question "Is Mormonism Christian?" is today one of the most frequently asked questions about this religion. But that hasn't always been the case. Mormons have been called many things since their movement emerged in the 1800s: superstitious, dupes, fanatics, power-hungry, barbaric. They're used to being accused by other Christian groups of misinterpreting the Bible – and Mormons have returned the accusation. Nevertheless, by the late twentieth century, Mormons had grown accustomed to being accepted under the umbrella of "Judeo-Christian" America. Indeed, at mid-twentieth century, century, Mormons were sometimes classified, against their own preference, as "Protestant" (as in the U.S. military, where the LDS pushed to be recognized as their own separate category). So when Mormons during the last quarter of the twentieth century faced a new barrage of challenges to their claim to be Christian, it came as rather a shock to them.

To Mormons, it seems obvious that they're Christians. Most Mormons assert that their movement is the same church established by Jesus himself, corrupted over the centuries but then restored in its purity through revelations to Joseph Smith Jr. Historically, then, Mormons have not only regarded theirs as a Christian church; they have regarded theirs as the only *true* Christian church. Whether we're talking about the LDS, the RLDS (now Community of Christ), or the FLDS, the name "Christ" appears in the denomination's name. Rites are performed in the name of Jesus Christ. Mormons are baptized, like other Christians. They regularly partake of bread and wine – or a non-alcoholic alternative – in memory of Christ's body and blood, like other Christians. They revere Jesus as the Son of God and the Savior of the world. Why would anyone think they're not Christian?

Arguments that Mormons aren't Christian come from basically two sources. One is ecumenical Christian churches. These are churches that in the pluralist climate of the post-1960s became interested in cooperating more closely with each other. Some Protestant churches talked about the possibility of merging, while Catholics took the more modest, yet historically important, step of formally recognizing Protestant baptisms. But ecumenical initiatives required greater clarity about who, exactly, counted as Christian and could therefore be part of these initiatives. Thus initiatives intended to promote unity among Christians also led, paradoxically, to the deliberate exclusion of certain groups. While ecumenically minded Protestants and Catholics were prepared to say that they shared a common faith with one another, they weren't so sure about groups like Christian Scientists, the Unification Church, or Mormons. During the last decades of the twentieth century, some ecumenical churches – including Methodists, Presbyterians, and Catholics – issued statements explaining that they did not regard Mormonism as belonging to the historic Christian tradition. (They had in mind the LDS specifically.) These churches were happy to cooperate with Mormons in civic or humanitarian endeavors, but they wouldn't, for instance, recognize a Mormon baptism as a properly Christian baptism.

Mormons might find the ecumenical churches' statements insulting, but they were more concerned about a different source of arguments against Mormonism being Christian. That source was evangelicals. Recall that "evangelical" refers to conservative-minded Protestants. Evangelical Protestants are more likely than liberal Protestants to believe that Jesus is divine, that faith in Jesus is the only path to salvation, and that the Bible is without error, with the result that evangelicals also tend to be traditionalist on questions of morality, such as disapproving homosexuality. Evangelicalism surged in the United States during the 1970s and 1980s, both numerically and in visibility as evangelicals became an important political force. During the same period, the LDS Church also was growing and becoming more visible. That fact alarmed evangelicals, since LDS teaching differed from evangelical teaching in key respects. Because of those differences, evangelicals did not regard Mormonism as truly Christian – which is to say that evangelicals didn't regard Mormonism as Christian, period. In the evangelicals' view, people who joined Mormonism thinking that they were joining a Christian church were in fact being led away to damnation. This concern led to sometimes strident efforts by evangelicals to warn the public not to be fooled by Mormons' claim to be Christian.

Mormons were vividly aware of evangelical anti-Mormonism. Evangelicals sparred with LDS missionaries, picketed outside LDS temples, and advertised screenings of anti-Mormon films. Sometimes Mormons encountered evangelical opposition on occasions when they tried to make common cause with evangelicals on political or moral issues. Like evangelicals, many LDS in the post-1960s period embraced the ideology of a Judeo-Christian America and were troubled by secularism. (Recall Romney's comment at the town hall meeting we quoted earlier: that "we need to have a person *of faith* lead the country.") But when LDS tried to ally with evangelical groups around these issues, they sometimes found themselves rebuffed on the grounds that they were not, in fact, Christian. The man who announced that he wouldn't vote for Mitt Romney because Romney wasn't Christian was likely an evangelical. As such, that man probably shared many of Romney's social and moral values; but because of their theological differences, he was unwilling to stand with Romney in the realm of politics.

What are the theological differences? There are three main objections that Christian groups raise to recognizing Mormonism as Christian:

- Mormons do not accept the doctrine of the Trinity, the teaching that God consists of three persons – Father, Son, and Holy Spirit – who are nevertheless, in a mysterious way, one being. Christian bishops declared the doctrine of the Trinity to be essential for Christian faith during the 300s; typically, both ecumenical and evangelical churches still hold that standard today.
- Mormons use scriptures beyond the Bible – most famously, the Book of Mormon. Evangelical critics often argue that the Mormon scriptures contradict the Bible. (Mormons, by contrast, see their distinctive scriptures as an extension of, or corroborating witness to, the revelations found in the Bible.)
- Mormons teach that in order to enter heaven, people need to perform certain rites, such as baptism, and make efforts to live righteously, in addition to asking God to forgive their sins by virtue of Jesus Christ's self-sacrifice. This teaching is at odds with the position held by evangelical Protestants: that salvation comes by grace alone. By this, evangelicals mean that salvation is in no way conditional on works performed by human beings; people can be saved *only* by trusting God to forgive them through Christ's self-sacrifice. Because Mormons do not teach this, evangelicals charge Mormonism with teaching a "false gospel," a distorted version of the Christian message. Many evangelicals have held that for the same reason, Catholicism is not truly Christian either.

For the purposes of this book, we're going to set aside the question of whether or not Mormons need to subscribe to these criteria in order to count as Christian. That's a question for theologians to debate. As historians, we have different interests. We want to understand how different streams within Mormonism developed in ways that made them more or less susceptible to these theological criticisms, and we want to understand what the consequences have been for the different Mormon streams.

EVOLVING THEOLOGIES: THE HISTORICAL LAYERS OF MORMONISM

To understand how Mormons' relationship to the American Christian mainstream has changed over time, it is useful to think of early Mormonism as developing in layers, one laid down on top of the other. Each layer made Mormonism more distinctive, and thus less like what Americans would tend to see as "normal" for a Christian movement. Eventually, different Mormon streams retained different layers. As a result, certain Mormon streams look more conventionally Christian – and thus more mainstream – than others.

1. THE KIRTLAND LAYER

During the early 1830s, Mormonism was headquartered in Kirtland, Ohio. It was already evident by that point that Mormons had their own quite distinctive interpretation of Christianity. Mormons had important traits in common with their Christian neighbors: they embraced the Bible as scripture; they sought forgiveness of their sins through Jesus Christ's self-sacrifice; they talked about God in a relatively traditional Trinitarian way as Father, Son, and Holy Spirit. But Mormonism also had these unique characteristics:

In addition to the Bible, Mormons accepted other books of scripture, starting with the Book of Mormon, which claimed to recount the history of a group of Israelites who migrated from Jerusalem to the Americas several centuries before the birth of Jesus. Among these migrants and their descendants, a series of prophets foretold Jesus's ministry back in Palestine – how he would suffer and die to save humanity from their sins. Jesus himself visited the Americas after his resurrection to show that the prophecies had been fulfilled and to organize his church. A few hundred years later, the people strayed from Jesus's teachings and turned against one another in a bloody civil war, the survivors of which, early Mormons believed, were the ancestors of the Native Americans. One of the last surviving followers of Jesus, a man named Mormon, wrote a religious history of his people on golden plates; Mormon then turned the record over to his son Moroni, who buried it for safekeeping before he died. Nearly 1500 years later, Moroni appeared to Joseph Smith Jr., as an angel, to show him where the record was buried. God gave Smith power to translate the plates, which were then published as the Book of Mormon.

The story of the Book of Mormon's miraculous production attracted converts because they saw it as tangible evidence that God was powerfully at work in the world, preparing the way for Jesus's second coming. While Smith's claims about how he produced the Book of Mormon were immediately controversial, the book's theological teachings were fairly conventional, in line with many American Protestants' beliefs about fallen human nature and the need to find salvation from sin through Jesus Christ.

THE BOOK OF MORMON: JESUS VISITS THE AMERICAS

This excerpt from the Book of Mormon portrays Jesus visiting a place called Bountiful, somewhere in the Americas, after he rose from the dead in Jerusalem.

And now it came to pass that there were a great multitude gathered together, of the people of Nephi, round about the temple which was in the land Bountiful . . .

And behold, they saw a man descending out of heaven; and he was clothed in a white robe, and he came down and stood in the midst of them . . .

He stretched forth his hand, and spake unto the people, saying, behold, I am Jesus Christ, of whom the prophets testified shall come into the world . . .

When Jesus had spoken these words, the whole multitude fell to the earth, for they remembered that it had been prophesied among them that Christ should shew himself unto them after his ascension into heaven.

And it came to pass that the Lord spake unto them saying, arise and come forth unto me, that ye may thrust your hands into my side, and also that ye may feel the prints of the nails in my hands, and in my feet, that ye may know that I am the God of Israel, and the God of the whole earth, and have been slain for the sins of the world.

Source: *The Book of Mormon* (New York: Penguin Books, 2008), 484–485. A reproduction of the 1840 edition. Excerpts edited for readability.

Beyond the Book of Mormon, Mormons added a volume called Doctrine and Covenants to their canon of scripture. Whereas the Book of Mormon was understood to be an ancient record translated by Joseph Smith Jr., Doctrine and Covenants contained revelations given directly to Smith to guide the new Mormon movement. Smith issued revelations throughout his life, so Doctrine and Covenants kept expanding as new revelations were added to the collection. These revelations, more so than the Book of Mormon, were the source of teachings that began to set Mormons apart from other Christian groups. One of the revelations in Doctrine and Covenants taught that heaven was divided into three different kingdoms representing different levels, or "degrees," of glory. Those people who were most faithful in keeping God's commandments would inherit the highest level (the celestial), while those who lived less faithfully would inherit a lower level (either the terrestrial or the telestial). However, the revelation taught, almost all people would inherit some degree of glory; only a few would be condemned forever to hell. This conception of the afterlife was a middle ground between two competing views in American Christianity: on the one hand, the teaching of a relatively small number of Universalists, who believed that everyone would eventually go to heaven, and on the other hand, the view accepted by most Protestants in the 1800s, that most of the world's people would end up in hell.

Another distinctive trait that developed during Mormonism's Kirtland period was an elaborate structure of priestly offices. In this,

Mormonism looked more Catholic than Protestant. The Mormon priesthood consisted of close to ten offices, organized into two tiers, the Aaronic priesthood and the Melchizedek priesthood, both of whose names were taken from the Bible. The Aaronic priesthood contained the offices of deacon, teacher, and priest, each with its own duties; the Melchizedek priesthood included the offices of elder, seventy, bishop, and high priest. Mormonism also had a council of Twelve Apostles (twelve high-ranking missionaries), a First Presidency (a three-member group to govern the whole church, consisting of Joseph Smith Jr. plus two councilors), and a Patriarch (also known as an evangelist, who had the function of pronouncing special blessings on individuals). This was a much more complex church organization than American Protestants were used to.

Another way in which Mormons differed from many other American Christian groups was in their distinctive understanding of sacred space: the temple. The first Mormon temple, built at Kirtland, was more than just a church as most Protestants would have understood it — more than just a convenient place to meet for worship. The temple was a place where God's presence and power would be revealed in a special way, through rites performed by priests. We will discuss the Mormon concept of temples in more detail in chapter 6.

2. THE NAUVOO LAYER

Because of conflicts in Ohio, Mormons moved their headquarters from Kirtland to Missouri. They then came into conflict with Missouri's government, leading them to build a new capital for their movement in Nauvoo, Illinois. While living in Nauvoo, in the last years before he was killed, Joseph Smith Jr. introduced teachings and rites that made Mormonism even more distinctive than it had been in the 1830s.

In Nauvoo, Smith introduced new teachings about the nature of God. He decisively broke with Trinitarianism, the mainstream Christian teaching that Father, Son, and Holy Spirit are three persons in one being. Smith taught instead that Father, Son, and Holy Spirit were three separate beings and that both the Father and the Son had physical bodies, made of flesh and bone. Smith therefore began to speak of Gods, in the plural. Furthermore, Smith taught, human beings were the same kind of being as God, although not as highly developed: human beings were Gods in embryonic form.

As this teaching solidified, Mormons were given the following picture of the cosmos. The being that humans know as God the Father was once a mortal human being himself, living, as we do, on some other earth. Through obedience to *his* God, he ascended to eternal glory, thus becoming a God himself. Our God then fathered the immortal spirits of every human being who has ever lived on our earth. This means that we are literally God's children: God is literally our Heavenly Father, with whom we lived, as spirits, in heaven before he sent us to be born into bodies here on earth. It follows logically that we also have a Heavenly Mother – a heretofore unknown being, God's wife, who gave birth to our immortal spirits in heaven. Jesus, like us, is one of God's spirit children, although Jesus is unique in that he is also God's only son on earth, through his supernatural conception by Mary. By obeying our Heavenly Father during his life on earth, Jesus himself advanced to become a God. In so doing, Jesus has given all of us a perfect model of how to live in order that we, too, may become Gods – in Smith's language, so that we may be "exalted."

In order to summarize Nauvoo-era Mormon teachings about God in a short, simple way, we have had to use language that is not always the language Mormons themselves use. For example, Mormons do not typically refer to the Heavenly Mother as "God's wife," an expression that might strike them as irreverent, even if it does accurately convey the concept. Mormons who accept these Nauvoo-era teachings tend to use more conventional language when talking about God in their day-to-day lives. Many Christians talk about God as our Father in heaven, or about human beings being brothers and sisters, or about human beings having been created in the image of God, or about trying to be more like God (for example, trying to love others the way God loves them). This is the language Mormons typically use as well. But Nauvoo-era Mormonism uses this conventional language to refer to decidedly less conventional concepts.

WHAT IS KOLOB?

A common perception is that Mormons believe "God lives on a planet called Kolob," to quote the comedic Broadway musical The Book of Mormon. *This way of describing Mormonism gives* it an air of science fiction, thereby associating Mormonism with more recent marginal religions involving extraterrestrials, such as Scientology, Raelians, or some forms of New Age spirituality.

In fact, in Mormon scripture Kolob is neither a planet nor God's home, but the first star that God created. (Mormon scripture offers no specifics about where God lives, beyond "heaven" or the "celestial kingdom.") Kolob is referred to in the Book of Abraham, which Joseph Smith Jr. published in Nauvoo. In the text, God gives Abraham a vision of the cosmos, including the following:

I, Abraham, . . . saw the stars also that they were very great, and that one of them was nearest unto the throne of God; and there were many great ones, which were near unto it; and the Lord said unto me, these are the governing ones; and the name of the great one is Kolob, because it is near unto me: for I am the Lord thy God, I have set this one . . . to govern all those planets which belong to the same order as that upon which thou standest. . . .

Thus I, Abraham, talked with the Lord, face to face, as one man talketh with another; and he told me of the works which his hands had made.

Source: "The Book of Abraham," *Times and Seasons*, March 15, 1842, 719. Available online as "The Book of Abraham, Early 1842," *The Joseph Smith Papers*, josephsmithpapers.org.

To achieve exaltation, it was necessary to perform certain ceremonies, which Smith introduced in Nauvoo. One of these ceremonies was the endowment. This ceremony was based partly on rites of Freemasonry, a fraternal organization Smith joined while in Nauvoo. Smith fused elements of Masonic rites to his new ideas about exaltation to create a ceremony in which participants were washed and anointed, like ancient priests, and received esoteric, or confidential, instructions that would prepare them to be exalted in the afterlife. Smith also introduced a marriage rite that "sealed" husbands and wives to one another through the power of God's Spirit, so that their unions would last not only during this life but after death, through all eternity. Men and women needed to be eternally married in this way in order to become Gods because, Smith taught, a key attribute of Godhood was the power to go on having children forever – like our Heavenly Father and Mother, who produced us as their spirit children. When Smith introduced the sealing rite in Nauvoo, he used it to create polygamous marriages by sealing the same man to more than one woman. Smith himself was sealed to perhaps more than thirty women this way, in secret. Polygamy – or "plural marriage," as Mormons called it – allowed a man to have a larger family in the afterlife, thereby increasing his and his wives' eternal joy. In addition to sealing husbands and wives, Mormons also sealed parents to children, thus linking generations into a constantly expanding eternal family.

As part of their effort to eternally link the generations, Mormons in Nauvoo began to perform rites on behalf of individuals who had died. Mormons believed that in order to enter heaven, people needed to be baptized by the proper authority, authority that had been lost for centuries until God restored it by sending angels to ordain Smith. What hope, then, was there for people who had died without having the opportunity to be baptized by the proper authority? Smith's solution was baptism for the dead, in which living individuals were baptized in the name of deceased individuals; the deceased, in the afterlife, thus had the opportunity to accept or reject this baptism performed on their behalf. Later, Mormons began to perform the endowment and sealing rites on behalf of deceased individuals as well, making it possible for those individuals to be exalted to Godhood.

Mormonism's collection of scriptures was expanded during the Nauvoo period to include documents that supported the new teachings and practices. Instructions by Smith about baptism for the dead were added to Doctrine and Covenants. In Nauvoo, Smith published the Book of Abraham, which, like the Book of Mormon, he said was a translation of lost scripture. The Book of Abraham taught about human beings' previous existence as spirits and described the earth's creation as having been carried out by a council of Gods.

Nauvoo-era teachings and practices often strike outsiders as unusual. But these teachings all had their basis in distinctive Mormon interpretations of the Bible and in cultural ideas common to early nineteenth-century America. The Bible refers to the polygamous marriages of figures such as Abraham, Jacob, Moses, and David. In a passage from the New Testament, the apostle Paul mentions people being baptized "for the dead." Smith developed his vision of human beings progressing to become Gods during an age when many Americans embraced notions of human progress or some kind of divine light or potential within human beings. Many American Christians were concerned with forming perfected families, as well as debating the structure and scope of the Christian heaven. Nauvoo Mormonism was born out of the same cultural matrix that produced these other manifestations of American Christianity. Nevertheless, many American Christians saw Nauvoo-era Mormonism as breaking sharply with Christian teachings about God and marriage.

3. THE UTAH LAYER

During the crisis produced by Joseph Smith Jr.'s violent death, it became clear that different Mormons had come to believe quite different things. Some of Smith's teachings during his last years at Nauvoo had been public, including the idea that God was an exalted man, baptism for the dead, and the Book of Abraham. But Smith had given other teachings secretly to an inner circle; these teachings included the endowment and, most importantly, plural marriage. Mormons inside the inner circle embraced a different kind of Mormonism than those outside the circle, who adhered to a religion closer to Kirtland-era Mormonism.

Brigham Young was a member of the inner circle. When he led his LDS followers west to Utah, he continued Smith's Nauvoo-era innovations. But Young also added his own innovations, creating yet another layer in Mormonism's development.

Young gave further twists to Smith's teachings about God. For one thing, Young clearly believed that God had plural wives. (Smith may also have believed that, but the evidence is unclear.) Furthermore, Young taught that God, after fathering our spirits in heaven, came to earth to live as Adam, bringing with him one of his plural wives, who became Eve. Thus not only are all human beings children of God in the sense that God is the father of our immortal *spirits*, as Smith taught, all human beings are *physically* descended from God as well because we can all trace our earthly genealogies back to Adam, who is God. This teaching of Young's is called the Adam–God doctrine.

Young also taught something known as blood atonement. This teaching was that some sins are so serious that Jesus's self-sacrifice

Farthest from the American Protestant mainstream

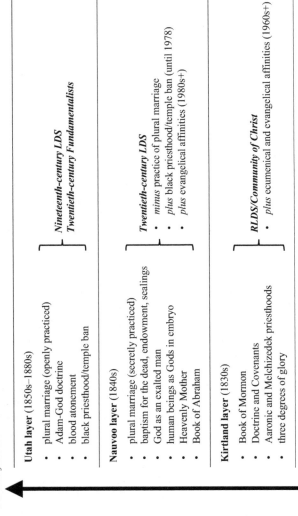

Utah layer (1850s–1880s)

- plural marriage (openly practiced)
- Adam–God doctrine
- blood atonement
- black priesthood/temple ban

Nineteenth-century LDS
Twentieth-century Fundamentalists

Nauvoo layer (1840s)

- plural marriage (secretly practiced)
- baptism for the dead, endowment, sealings
- God as an exalted man
- human beings as Gods in embryo
- Heavenly Mother
- Book of Abraham

Twentieth-century LDS

- *minus* practice of plural marriage
- *plus* black priesthood/temple ban (until 1978)
- *plus* evangelical affinities (1980s+)

Kirtland layer (1830s)

- Book of Mormon
- Doctrine and Covenants
- Aaronic and Melchizedek priesthoods
- three degrees of glory

RLDS/Community of Christ

- *plus* ecumenical and evangelical affinities (1960s+)

Closest to the American Protestant mainstream

Figure 2.2 The three layers of Mormonism, with the Mormon streams, which retained each layer. As in archaeology, the oldest layer is at the bottom. Each successive layer adds new elements to the layer beneath.

is not enough to atone for them; individuals who commit these sins must atone for them by spilling their own blood. This teaching terrified some LDS, who understood it as a death threat against disobedient members of the movement. Preaching about blood atonement was most prominent during the 1850s, during a period of very tense conflict between the LDS and the federal government; after that it was muted.

A much longer-lasting teaching of Young's was that black Africans were a cursed race who were therefore ineligible to hold the priesthood or receive temple rites, including sealing and the endowment. Because the curse was hereditary, Young taught, people of other races should not intermarry with blacks. By barring people of black African ancestry from the temple, LDS leaders were barring them from rites necessary for exaltation and thus barring them from Godhood, at least until some future time when God might lift the curse. This was a form of racial exclusion without parallel among other white American Christians of the period. Many white Protestants in the South had embraced some variation of the idea that blacks inherited a biblical curse in order to justify African American slavery, and racial segregation was common in churches, both North and South. But few white Protestants would have denied that blacks could experience all the blessings of salvation in heaven, which was in effect what the LDS were teaching.

To sum up: By the end of the 1800s, Mormonism had developed three layers, as Smith or subsequent leaders introduced new teachings or rites. Each successive layer – Kirtland, Nauvoo, Utah – made Mormonism look more unconventional by American Protestant standards. In other words, each layer took Mormonism farther from the American Christian mainstream. But not all three streams of Mormonism embraced, or retained, attributes of all three layers. As a result, the three streams developed different relationships to the American Christian mainstream.

THE THREE STREAMS OF MORMONISM AND THE AMERICAN CHRISTIAN MAINSTREAM

Those Mormons who rejected Brigham Young's leadership and formed the Reorganization under the leadership of Joseph Smith III either did not know about Smith's secretive Nauvoo innovations, or they knew about those innovations and rejected them. The Reorganization thus rejected the Nauvoo layer of Mormonism in favor of the Kirtland layer. Joseph Smith III denied adamantly that his father had taught or practiced plural marriage, despite all evidence to the contrary. The Reorganization did not practice the endowment or rites of sealing, not even to seal monogamous marriages for eternity. Public Nauvoo-era teachings such as God being an exalted man or baptism for the dead were downplayed and gradually abandoned. For instance, Joseph Smith Jr.'s teachings about baptism for the dead appeared in the RLDS Doctrine and Covenants for most of the twentieth century; but the church maintained that these teachings were intended only for those living in Nauvoo at that time, and that baptism for the dead should not be practiced again unless God gave a new revelation to that effect. Near the end of the twentieth century, texts on baptism for the dead were removed from the RLDS Doctrine and Covenants altogether. Unlike the LDS, the RLDS never accepted the Book of Abraham as scripture.

Because they rejected Mormonism's Nauvoo layer, not to mention the Utah layer laid down by Brigham Young, the Reorganization looked more like mainstream American Christianity than the LDS did. Certainly the RLDS retained Mormon hallmarks that set them off from other Christian groups: the Book of Mormon, Doctrine and Covenants, the Aaronic and Melchizedek priesthoods and all of the offices and councils associated with them. But by making clear that they did not accept polygamy or other Nauvoo- or Utah-layer elements, the RLDS avoided the intense opposition that the LDS in Utah experienced during the last half of the 1800s. Whatever differences the RLDS might have from the Christian mainstream, other Americans weren't much worried about them.

The LDS, by contrast, continued to be attacked by America's Protestant majority — not violently, as had happened back in the 1830s, but in the press and in the form of government efforts to stamp out polygamy. Protestant critics abhorred polygamy as uncivilized and un-Christian; they associated the practice with Islam or traditional African societies. That view was echoed by the U.S. Supreme Court when the justices upheld anti-polygamy laws as constitutional on the grounds that polygamy was "contrary to the spirit of Christianity and of the civilization which Christianity has produced in the Western world." The anti-polygamy campaign was one way in which white Anglo-Saxon Protestants moved during the late nineteenth and early twentieth centuries to ensure that their values would dominate American society. That same historical period saw intensifying anti-Catholicism and anti-Semitism, bans on Asian immigration and restrictive quotas on the immigration of other non-Anglo-Saxon groups, and sensationalistic journalism about new or newly planted religious movements such as schools of Hinduism.

When the LDS suspended the practice of polygamy at the turn of the twentieth century, they began a process of accommodation to mainstream American norms that resulted in their retreating from aspects of the Utah layer of Mormonism. LDS leaders distanced themselves from Brigham Young's Adam-God doctrine and his teachings about blood atonement, some going so far as to deny that Young had actually taught these things. However, a very important element of the Utah layer persisted: the ban on blacks receiving the priesthood or temple rites remained in effect until the late twentieth century.

Apart from suspending the practice of polygamy and retaining the black priesthood/temple ban, the LDS in the twentieth century embraced the Nauvoo layer of Mormonism: God as an exalted man and the possibility of Godhood for human beings; Heavenly Mother; baptism for the dead, the endowment, and sealings; and the Book of Abraham, which the LDS incorporated into a thin volume called the Pearl of Great Price, a fourth work of scripture alongside the Bible, the Book of Mormon, and Doctrine and Covenants. However, Nauvoo-layer aspects of LDS religion were not necessarily visible to outsiders. Baptism for the dead, the endowment, and sealings were performed in temples and were therefore not open to public view. Heavenly Mother was rarely talked about because the subject was considered sacred, although LDS congregations sang a beloved hymn referring to her that dated back to Nauvoo days. And as we noted earlier, the LDS often used conventional biblical language when talking about God or exaltation (since the LDS understood these concepts as biblical), so outsiders might not recognize that the LDS used this language in a distinctive way. By the middle of the twentieth century, the LDS were widely accepted, despite their persistent peculiarities, as part of America's "Judeo-Christian" mainstream. The Mormon Tabernacle Choir, for example, had a very long-running radio and then television program, broadcast around the nation from Salt Lake City every Sunday morning, during which they sang Christian hymns and a speaker delivered a generically Judeo-Christian sermonette.

What of the third Mormon stream, the Fundamentalists? With the disclaimer that Fundamentalist groups differ among themselves, the kind of Mormonism practiced by Fundamentalists through the twentieth century and beyond most closely resembled the Utah layer of the late nineteenth century. What the LDS retreated from, the Fundamentalists kept: plural marriage, the Adam-God doctrine, and teachings justifying the black priesthood/temple ban, the lifting of which by the LDS in 1978 became one more sign, for Fundamentalists, that LDS leaders had gone astray. In fringe cases, Fundamentalists invoked the blood atonement doctrine to justify murder. (See chapter 3.)

When we examined the bigger picture of religious pluralism and Christian dominance in U.S. history, we saw examples of religious minorities, such as Jews and Buddhists, adopting language or practices that made them look more like the Protestant majority. Mormonism presents a similar pattern: both the Reorganization and the LDS avoided opposition from the Protestant majority by retreating from teachings and practices that made them stand out from Protestants. The LDS remained more distinctive than the Reorganization did because the LDS retained more from Mormonism's Nauvoo layer, but those Nauvoo-era traits may not have been all that visible to outsiders. For instance, people watching the Sunday broadcasts of the Mormon Tabernacle Choir may have perceived LDS to be more conventional in their religious beliefs and practices than they actually were.

That situation changed during the last quarter of the twentieth century, as both ecumenical churches and evangelical Protestants paid more attention to the LDS Church's Nauvoo-layer teachings as grounds for declaring that LDS religion did not meet those churches' definitions of Christianity. LDS responded by becoming even more cautious about using language that they feared might strike outsiders as weird, such as people "becoming Gods." The LDS Church became more conspicuously Christ-centered in its image and messaging, such as adopting a new logo in which the words "Jesus Christ" were literally enlarged in the church's name, or having missionaries place greater emphasis on Christ in their teaching, so that no one could mistake theirs for anything other than a Christian church. At the same time, the way that LDS themselves understood their religion took on certain affinities with evangelical Protestantism as a result of popular LDS devotional writers reading and absorbing ideas from evangelical writers, such as the British evangelical C.S. Lewis (best known for writing the Narnia series for children) or the American evangelical pastor John MacArthur (who ironically was also a prominent evangelical critic of Mormonism). LDS at the end of the twentieth century talked more frequently about being saved "by grace" than they had through most of the nineteenth and twentieth centuries; back then, LDS leaders had condemned Protestant teachings about salvation by grace for excusing moral laxity and distorting scriptural teaching about the need to keep God's commandments. By contrast, LDS at the turn of the twenty-first century developed a new-found love for decidedly evangelical hymns such as "Amazing Grace." LDS religion was still Nauvoo-layer Mormonism, but with more of an evangelical tone to it.

WHY DON'T MORMONS USE CROSSES?

Early Mormons didn't adorn their churches with crosses because in the early 1800s most American Protestants didn't adorn their churches with crosses; that was viewed as a Catholic practice. Crosses became much more common in Protestant architecture, jewelry, and so on as the 1800s progressed. Mormons, however, continued to associate the cross with movements other than their own. Some Mormons developed quite hostile attitudes toward the cross, seeing it as a symbol of the corrupted Christianity that their movement was meant to correct.

As liberal RLDS reoriented themselves toward mainline Protestantism in the late twentieth century, they came to use crosses more frequently. Today, a large cross adorns the exterior of Community of Christ's Temple in Independence. Among the LDS, antipathy toward crosses shows some signs of softening at the individual level, but the church still avoids the symbol at the institutional level. The LDS are much more likely to use as symbols of their movement the angel Moroni, who tops the steeples of most temples, or the Christus, a white marble statue of the resurrected Jesus (copied, ironically, from the national cathedral of Denmark's Protestant state church).

Read more: Michael G. Reed, *Banishing the Cross: The Emergence of a Mormon Taboo* (Independence, MO: John Whitmer Books, 2012).

The Reorganization underwent a yet more dramatic transformation during the same period. Starting in the 1960s, RLDS leaders in the United States began attending mainstream Protestant seminaries for theological training. As a result, RLDS teaching absorbed language and ideas characteristic of ecumenical churches. Many RLDS came to regard their church not as the one true church, but as one among many authentically Christian denominations. Use of the Book of Mormon declined sharply in favor of the Bible. Certain other distinctively Mormon teachings that the Reorganization had retained up to that point, such as the three degrees of glory, declined as well. Not all RLDS approved of these developments: as this more ecumenical style of Mormonism became the norm in the RLDS Church, those who rejected the changes broke away to form what became known as Restorationist communities. At the same time, as the RLDS Church grew internationally, many of its members outside the United States embraced forms of worship and theological outlooks that resembled evangelicalism or Pentecostalism. We'll discuss that development more in chapter 7; for now, the point to take away is that by the beginning of the twenty-first century, the RLDS Church had developed new affinities with both evangelicalism and the ecumenical churches. These shifts in the church's identity were reflected in the decision to change the church's name from "the Reorganized Church of Jesus Christ of Latter Day Saints" to "Community of Christ." The change indicated that this stream of Mormonism had become even less invested in Mormon hallmarks, and that its members increasingly saw themselves as *a* community of Christ, not *the* community of Christ. Of the various Mormon streams, Community of Christ had moved closest to the American Christian mainstream.

They became, as it were, card-carrying members of the mainstream when in 2010 Community of Christ was accepted as a member of the National Council of Churches, a leading ecumenical body in the United States.

Fundamentalists remained farthest from the religious mainstream. Where the LDS and RLDS sought at the end of the twentieth century to be recognized as Christian, Fundamentalists faced a bigger problem: convincing the public they were not a "cult." Evangelical Protestants had used that four-letter word since the beginning of the twentieth century to describe movements they regarded as not authentically Christian – from Catholics, to Christian Scientists, to the LDS. By the end of the twentieth century, the term was used more broadly by Americans to refer to religious movements perceived as bizarre to the point of dangerous: irrational and oppressive. (Recall that the religious majority in America has been voicing concerns about reputedly irrational or oppressive religious minorities since the early 1800s.) The LDS sometimes found themselves labeled a cult, but the Fundamentalists were even more vulnerable to the label. Perceptions that the FLDS Church was a cult fueled support for the government raid on the FLDS community in Eldorado, Texas, in 2008, when the state seized custody of over 400 FLDS children, an action later overturned by the courts as government overreach. American society had become more pluralist, but the labeling of groups like the FLDS as "cults" indicated where the limits of religious freedom still lay for many Americans.

CONCLUSION

Americans take pride in their country's tradition of religious freedom. Yet groups outside the Protestant mainstream have struggled over the course of American history to gain equality – or in some cases, simply the right to exist in the United States. Religious minorities whom Protestants perceived as threatening were subjected to prejudiced depictions in the media, legal restrictions, and at times violence. Mormons are one such religious minority.

The question of whether or not Mormonism is Christian – or worse, whether or not Mormonism is a cult – is a question of whether or not Mormons can claim mainstream status in the United States. Can Mormons participate equally in American society? Can a Mormon be president? At the beginning of the twenty-first century, the answer to such questions still depends partly on how far other Americans perceive Mormons to be from a presumed religious "norm." Different Mormon streams stand closer or farther to the mainstream based on whether the teachings and practices they embrace set them apart more or less dramatically from Protestantism. Community of Christ is closest. Fundamentalists are farthest away. The LDS stand somewhere in between.

SUGGESTIONS FOR FURTHER READING

Philip L. Barlow, *Mormons and the Bible: The Place of Latter-day Saints in American Religion*, 2nd ed. (New York: Oxford University Press, 2013).

J. Spencer Fluhman, *A Peculiar People: Anti-Mormonism and the Making of Religion in Nineteenth-Century America* (Chapel Hill: University of North Carolina Press, 2012).

Paul C. Gutjar, *The Book of Mormon: A Biography* (Princeton, NJ: Princeton University Press, 2012).

J. B. Haws, *The Mormon Image in the American Mind: Fifty Years of Public Perception* (New York: Oxford University Press, 2013).

Gordon Shepherd and Gary Shepherd, *A Kingdom Transformed: Early Mormonism and the Modern LDS Church* (Salt Lake City: University of Utah Press, 2015).

Jan Shipps, "Joseph Smith and the Creation of LDS Theology," and "Is Mormonism Christian? Reflections on a Complicated Question," in *Sojourner in the Promised Land: Forty Years among the Mormons* (Urbana: University of Illinois Press, 2000), 289–301, 335–357.

3

BUILDING GOD'S KINGDOM

MORMONS AND CHURCH–STATE RELATIONS

On March 30, 2008, Flora Jessop received an unexpected call from a stranger. The caller, who identified herself as a 16-year-old girl named Sarah, whispered into the phone in a frightened voice. Sarah said that she had been locked into a boarded-up room at a Texas ranch and repeatedly assaulted by an older man to whom she had been assigned as a polygamous wife by FLDS church leaders. Sarah was calling for help. Jessop, an ex-member of the FLDS and founder of a group called Help the Child Brides, hastily contacted Texas authorities. The state was quick to act. On April 3, dozens of law enforcement officials, including snipers and an armored personnel carrier, stormed the Yearning for Zion Ranch in Eldorado, Texas, the site of an FLDS community and temple. Officials removed 400 children and teens from the ranch, claiming protective custody of them as the state investigated the caller's charges.

In the days that followed, news outlets across the United States broadcast pictures of women and children boarding buses, separated by authorities from their fathers, husbands, and patriarchal leaders. "The message from Texas is that we're not going to allow older men to sexually assault or commit rape of minors or marry minors here," proclaimed Texas state representative Harvey Hilderbran, who had previously sponsored legislation targeting the FLDS community in Eldorado.[1] Meanwhile, mothers of the children appeared on television programs like *Good Morning America* to provide their side of the story. Clad in their distinctive prairie-style dresses, the women pleaded to have their children back, arguing that the government had violated their constitutional rights. "We were taken at gunpoint without any explanation. There was no paper served. We were like animals, herded, and our children were taken," said one visibly shaken mother.[2]

As media scrutiny intensified, the accusation that had prompted the raid began to unravel. "Sarah," supposedly a child bride at the ranch, turned out to be a mentally unstable woman in Colorado who had never had any association with the FLDS. Public opinion began to turn against the state, now accused of abusing its own power. As a lawyer with the American Civil Liberties Union told a reporter, "Of course, we condemn child abuse," but "what the state has done has offended a pretty wide swath of the American people with what appears to be an overreaching action to sweep up all these children."[3] An appeals court agreed, ruling that the state of Texas did not have appropriate grounds to take all of the community's children into custody. Subsequently, FLDS parents were reunited with their children. Still, the state of Texas continued its investigation of the FLDS community's polygamous practices. That investigation led to over 100 FLDS adults being declared guilty of complicity in child abuse, with several men sentenced to prison for having sexual relationships with underage teens.

From an FLDS perspective, this drama was history repeating itself. From the beginning of the movement, Mormons had repeatedly been persecuted by outsiders, often with government assistance. During the late 1800s, LDS communities had been raided by federal officials determined to stamp out polygamy. Then, during the first half of the twentieth century, the Fundamentalist community at Short Creek had been raided. For the Mormons involved, these were simple cases of the government denying them their constitutional right to practice their religion. Mormon polygamy required the Supreme Court to rule, for the first time in U.S. history, on the meaning of that right. Americans took pride in a heritage of religious freedom. But did that freedom have limits, and where should they be drawn? If a law clashed with the teachings of a religious minority, should the religious minority be exempt from that law? Could American society tolerate a religious group that regarded obeying God as a higher value than obeying government? Mormonism is one of a number of minority religions that have pressed Americans to face complicated questions about how church and state – religion and government – relate in their country.

In this chapter, you'll read about:

- A bigger picture: church–state relations in early America.
- Church–state conflicts around early Mormonism.
- The Mormon streams part ways on church–state relations.
- LDS political involvement in the twentieth and twenty-first centuries.
- A glance at Mormons and the state outside the United States.

A BIGGER PICTURE: CHURCH–STATE RELATIONS IN EARLY AMERICA

It's often said that America was founded by people who came look-ing for religious freedom. That statement is partly true. A number of religious groups did migrate to the English colonies that later became the United States because they were escaping persecution or second-class citizenship back in Europe. But there were restrictions on religious freedom in the colonies, too. Most of the English colo-nies (nine out of thirteen) had a religious establishment, meaning a state-supported church. It was common in the colonies for certain religious minorities – Jews or Catholics, for instance – to be legally barred from voting or holding government office. Also, religious minorities could be required to pay taxes to support the state church, even though it wasn't their church.

After the American Revolution, religious minorities in the newly formed United States pushed back against religious establishments. States with religious establishments began abolishing them, a process that was still not quite complete when Mormonism began. (When the first Mormon congregation was formally organized in 1830, Massachusetts was the one state that still had a tax-supported church left over from colonial days.) Meanwhile, at the federal level, reli-gious minorities successfully lobbied for the First Amendment to the Constitution, which forbade Congress from creating a religious establishment or from prohibiting the "free exercise" of religion.

These were dramatic changes in American church–state relations; the United States was a pioneer among Western nations in rolling back religious establishments. However, even under the new American system, religions were still limited in important ways in their relations with the government. By the time Mormonism emerged in the 1830s, the following principles had become the dominant thinking in the United States about church–state relations:

1. THE STATE IS SUPREME OVER RELIGION

This principle had been a defining ideal of the Protestant Reformation back in England. You've probably heard about Henry VIII wanting to divorce his wife and being denied permission by the Pope. Henry responded by getting Parliament to declare that the king (or queen) of England, not the Pope, was the head of the church in England. This meant that Henry was now free to divorce his wife. It also meant that under English law, the state held supreme authority in religious matters. The state, for example, had the power to decide what creeds or forms of worship English subjects were required to follow, and the state had the power to decide whether or not to exempt religious minorities from that requirement. Before Henry VIII's time, during the medieval era, there had been other power struggles between popes and kings over who held supreme authority: church (popes) or state (kings). In England, as in other European nations that turned Protestant, the struggle was decided in favor of the state.

The principle of state supremacy over religion persisted in the American colonies and then the new United States. Even voices who advocated greater freedom for religious minorities – voices like William Penn, founder of Pennsylvania, or Thomas Jefferson – were careful to specify that religious freedom should not be understood as freedom to defy the authority of the state. Members of minority religions, Penn and Jefferson insisted, could be tolerated *as long as they were law-abiding subjects.* When Americans ended religious establishments after the Revolution, they ended direct government support of particular churches; they also ended certain kinds of legal restrictions on minority religions, like the laws that kept Jews or Catholics out of government. But Americans did not reject the English Protestant principle of state supremacy over religion.

The state-supremacy principle has two corollaries that are important for understanding the story of Mormons' relationship to the state:

1A. THE STATE HOLDS A MONOPOLY ON VIOLENCE

In other words, only agents of the state – such as the police or the military – are authorized to use physical force against someone, imprison someone, or kill someone. If anyone does those things without the state's authorization, it's a crime. That principle may seem common sense. But over the course of U.S. history, there have been religious groups who believed that God had authorized them to use violence, contrary to the state: African Americans revolting violently against slavery; Christians who assassinated abortion providers to protect the unborn; Muslims who plotted attacks against what they saw as a morally corrupt and oppressive U.S. government. The state has used violent force to shut down these religious exercises of violence – not because the state is opposed to violence but because the state is opposed to anyone other than itself using violence.

1B. DUTY TO THE STATE TRUMPS DUTY TO GOD

Although Americans talk about being a nation "under God," the practical reality is that if you believe the state's laws conflict with God's laws, the state will expect you to put its laws first. In other words, the state decides what people are allowed to do in the name of religious freedom. For people in the religious majority, this typically isn't a problem: the state's laws won't conflict with the values of the religious majority if the majority rules. But minority religious groups are more likely to find themselves in situations where they feel forced to choose between obedience to their religion and obedience to the state. If the religious minority is fortunate, the state may decide to grant them an exemption from the law, or at least look the other way if they don't obey it. If they're not so fortunate, the minority will face a difficult dilemma.

2. CHURCH AND STATE SHOULD BE SEPARATE

This principle has become controversial in recent decades for reasons we'll discuss later. But up until the 1960s, most Americans – Protestants especially – would not have hesitated to say that church and state should be separate. What they meant by this was that there shouldn't be state churches. They also meant, typically, that religious authorities shouldn't exercise state authority; in other words, priests or ministers shouldn't dictate how the government was run.

This principle grew partly out of religious minorities' resentments about the restrictions they had faced under colonial establishments. But the principle also owed much to Protestants' fears about Catholicism. Many American Protestants of the 1800s (and some American Protestants today) regarded the Catholic Church as a tyrannical institution. In Protestants' eyes, Catholic leaders demanded absolute obedience from their followers, opposed freedom of thought and expression, and aspired to use the power of the state to impose Catholic beliefs on society at large. This was not an entirely paranoid perception: during the 1800s, Catholic authorities in Europe did often support Catholic religious establishments and often preferred absolute monarchies over democracies to ensure social order. On the other hand, Catholics and other religious minorities in the United States complained that American Protestants showed no compunction about using the power of the state to impose *Protestant* values on society.

The number of Catholics living in nineteenth-century America swelled as a result of immigration. This led many Protestants to fear that Catholics, led by their priests, would use their voting power to win control of the government, bestow greater privileges and power on the Catholic Church, and ultimately dismantle constitutional law. In rallying around the principle of church–state separation, Protestants were rallying against the perceived threat that a tyrannical form of religion could subvert freedom and democracy. Protestants' solution to that threat was to insist that religious authority be kept a safe distance from state authority. Catholics were the principal focus of this concern during the 1800s. But Mormons were another.

CHURCH–STATE CONFLICTS AROUND EARLY MORMONISM

Early Mormonism clashed with American Protestants' notions about church–state relations. Mormons aspired to create the kingdom of God on earth. Protestants talked about doing that too, but Mormons understood "kingdom" more literally than most Protestants. For Mormons, building the kingdom meant gathering together to create theocratic communities, communities ruled by God. Mormon converts left their hometowns to form new settlements, which were meant to be holy communities, governed in all aspects by God's law as revealed in the scriptures and to Joseph Smith Jr., the living prophet.

Other religious groups had similar aspirations – the Amish, for example. But unlike the Amish, Mormons voted. Mormons ran for political office. Mormons' ideas about how to be a holy community did not preclude their participating in the state, and that's where things became problematic. The terms on which Mormons wanted to participate in the state clashed with the way that the majority of Americans thought religions should relate to the state.

CHURCH–STATE SEPARATION

In Mormon communities, religious authority and state authority overlapped – some observers would say they became fused. Mormon leaders exercised authority not only over "churchly" matters like creeds, morals, or forms of worship. Mormon leaders also ran their community's economy or told Mormons which political candidates they should vote for to protect their community's interests. Mormons voted their church leaders into positions in local government. In Nauvoo, Illinois, the Saints' central community during the early 1840s, Joseph Smith Jr. was simultaneously mayor, chief judge, and head of a Mormon militia.

Mormons who supported this kind of church–state overlap – not all did – regarded it as perfectly natural. For these Mormons, their religion wasn't just about where they went to church on Sunday or how they organized their private lives. In their effort to build holy communities, Mormons looked to church leadership to govern all aspects of their community life, economics and politics included, through revelation from God. This theocratic ideal clashed, however, with the American Protestant vision of church–state separation. Protestants – and those Mormons who came to oppose theocracy – regarded Mormon leaders as wielding tyrannical power. When Mormon communities became large enough to politically dominate a region, the perceived threat of tyranny became more alarming. If Mormons could vote their leaders into power, would non-Mormons find themselves forced to do the will of Mormon leaders? When Joseph Smith Jr. announced in 1844 that he was running for U.S. president, this bolstered critics' perceptions of the Mormon prophet as a would-be dictator who aspired to be obeyed not just by a church but by the entire nation.

We should note that Mormons who embraced the theocratic ideal saw no contradiction with the U.S. Constitution. They hailed the Constitution as inspired by God to protect people's liberties. They appealed to the Constitution's guarantee of religious freedom for the right to organize their communities as they deemed best. They professed to support religious freedom for all, even as they envisioned a future in which Jesus would rule the world through their church. Contradictory or naïve as this might look to outsiders, Mormons did not perceive themselves to be at odds with American values.

STATE SUPREMACY

Mormons sent mixed messages about whether they regarded the state's authority as supreme. On the one hand, Joseph Smith Jr. wrote in what came to be known as the Articles of Faith that Mormons believed "in being subject to kings, presidents, rulers, and magistrates, in obeying, honoring, and sustaining the law." On the other hand, Smith and some other Mormons regarded themselves as divinely authorized to operate outside the law. Polygamy is the prime example: Mormons practiced it in violation of the law, on the grounds that obedience to God's commandments was more important than obedience to the state.

Early Mormons also rejected the state's monopoly on violence. When Missourians opposed to growing Mormon political power launched violent attacks on Mormon communities, Smith announced that he had received revelations instructing Mormons to take up arms to defend themselves. The result was a small-scale civil war between Mormons and non-Mormons in the fall of 1838. The conflict ended when the governor of Missouri authorized the state militia to "exterminate" Mormons if they didn't leave the state. Smith and other Mormon leaders were charged with treason – in essence, with rejecting the state's authority. Six years later, when Smith was killed in an Illinois jail, he was there, again, on fresh charges of treason.

Mormons insisted that they used violence in self-defense: they had to protect themselves because the state had failed to protect them. It is true that in the Missouri conflict, Mormons suffered the worst violence, including an atrocity known as the Haun's Mill massacre, when a large non-Mormon militia force shot down almost twenty men and boys at a small Mormon settlement. But Mormons' willingness to resort to violence, coupled to the perception that Mormons regarded themselves as above earthly law, helped the movement's enemies paint Mormons as dangerous. This perception led to the Mormons' expulsion from Missouri and then from Nauvoo.

The same period in U.S. history that saw violence against Mormons, the 1830s–1840s, also saw mob violence against Catholics. Mormonism and Catholicism were both perceived among American Protestants as tyrannical religions that rejected American ideals of church–state relations and thus threatened other Americans' freedoms.

THE MORMON STREAMS PART WAYS ON CHURCH–STATE RELATIONS

Following the death of Joseph Smith Jr., Mormons responded in different ways to the pressure to conform to the church–state ideals that dominated American society. Let's look at the courses taken by the Reorganization, the LDS, and the Fundamentalists.

THE REORGANIZATION AND THE STATE

Church–state separation: The Reorganization retreated quickly from theocracy and armed violence. As prophet-president of the RLDS Church, Joseph Smith III counseled his followers to stop gathering to form their own settlements; instead, he advised that they should build up God's kingdom in a more metaphorical sense by growing congregations in the communities where they already lived. Some RLDS gathered anyway, into a communitarian settlement in Iowa they named Lamoni (after a pacifist king in the Book of Mormon). But Joseph Smith III kept that community-building project at arm's length; he did not govern Lamoni the way his father had governed Nauvoo. Nor did Joseph Smith III encourage his followers to vote *en bloc* or organize them into a military force, as his father had done.

As a result, the RLDS never had the political strength that Mormons achieved in Missouri and Illinois during the 1830s–1840s, which meant in turn that the RLDS did not seem threatening to their neighbors. They were a "safe" religious minority. Furthermore, the RLDS Church used a democratic style of governance, in which church policy was voted on by delegates from the congregations, not simply handed down from the highest levels. Even revelations to the church's prophet-president had to be accepted by a majority vote of delegates – and although the vote was always in favor, usually by overwhelming margins, it was understood that conceivably a majority might decide that a purported revelation was not, in fact, the will of God. This principle of democracy in church governance, familiar to Protestants, made RLDS leaders less likely to be perceived by non-Mormons as tyrannical.

State supremacy: The Reorganization emphatically rejected polygamy, to the point of denying that Joseph Smith Jr. ever taught or practiced it; the RLDS maintained that polygamy was Brigham Young's invention. Consequently, the Reorganization didn't come into conflict with the state over polygamy as the LDS did. To the contrary, the RLDS tried to enlist the state to support their claim that they, not the LDS, were the true successors of the movement founded by Joseph Smith Jr. Around 1880, the RLDS Church went to court hoping to resolve the legally murky question of who owned the temple that the Mormons had built in Kirtland, Ohio, half a century earlier. The RLDS Church argued that it was entitled to own the temple because it had remained true to the original doctrines of Mormonism, whereas the polygamous LDS Church had deviated from those doctrines. The LDS, 1500 miles away in Utah, were probably unaware of the case and therefore didn't send representatives to make counterarguments; the judge ended up dismissing the case on a technicality. However, because the RLDS Church's arguments were entered into the legal record, many RLDS believed that the courts had recognized them as the authentic successors of Joseph Smith Jr. These RLDS felt validated by this supposed stamp of approval from the state.

Another way that the Reorganization recognized the supreme authority of the state was by retreating from the militarism that Mormons had practiced in Missouri and Illinois. "Peace" became the official motto of the RLDS Church, symbolized on the church's seal by a child standing with a harmless lion and a lamb, a reference to a biblical prophecy about the lion and the lamb lying down together in harmony. Contrary to the impression that motto might give, the RLDS were not pacifists: they did not reject the legitimacy of war, the way some Christian groups, known as "peace churches," did.

Members of peace churches refused to fight if their country went to war. RLDS, by contrast, were willing to serve in the military. In two senses, then, the Reorganization consented to the state's monopoly on violence: unlike Mormons of the 1830s–1840s, RLDS would not fight without the state's authorization; but if the state led the nation into war, RLDS would follow.

THE LDS AND THE STATE

Church–state separation: After being forced to leave Nauvoo under threat of violence, the LDS migrated outside what were then the borders of the United States, to the Intermountain West. There they made a more ambitious attempt to build God's kingdom on earth than anything Mormons had tried up until then. More than just a city, the LDS set out to create an entire state, named Deseret (a word from the Book of Mormon said to mean "honeybee"). Deseret was a theocratic state: church leaders served as the state government; congregations doubled as "wards," a unit of city government; and bishops, the leaders of congregations, also sat as judges to resolve legal disputes.

Deseret was short-lived, however, because after the Mexican-American War of 1846–1848, the U.S. government claimed possession of the land where the LDS lived. Deseret became the Utah Territory, and U.S. officials began imposing Protestant expectations about church–state separation. As non-Mormon immigration to Utah increased through the latter half of the 1800s, the LDS tried to preserve some sense of a separate, theocratic society by creating parallel institutions governed by church leadership: church schools, church-owned businesses and industries, a church-run political party. LDS missionaries encouraged their converts to gather to the kingdom of God in Utah; this influx of LDS immigrants kept LDS voting power strong.

The LDS believed that the rights of self-government granted to states by the U.S. Constitution should have allowed their theocratic state to be admitted to the Union; but America's Protestant majority would not allow that. Before Utah could join the United States, the LDS had to abandon their theocratic institutions. As they had during Joseph Smith Jr.'s lifetime, Protestants continued to equate Mormon theocracy with tyranny. In a best-selling book of the 1880s, one Protestant minister objected that leaders in the LDS Church claimed "the right to control in all things religious, social, industrial and political. . . . Mormonism, therefore, is not simply a church, but a state; an '*imperium in imperio*' [a state within a state] ruled by a man who is prophet, priest, king and pope, all in one."[4]

The LDS finally gave up their theocratic aspirations at the end of the 1800s, thus clearing the way for Utah to be admitted to the United States in 1896. Many of the church's schools were turned over to the state to become public schools. Church leaders stopped trying to maintain a separate LDS economy, although the church retained extensive property and business holdings. The church's political party was dissolved, the LDS redistributed themselves into the Republican and Democratic parties, and church leaders became very cautious about making statements that would suggest they were "meddling" in politics. Within the church, governance was still hierarchical rather than democratic: church policies were decided by top-ranking leaders, in their capacity as living prophets, and then handed down to congregations, without the kind of voting-by-delegates seen in the Reorganization. In this, the LDS Church resembled the Catholic Church, while the Reorganization resembled the major Protestant churches. But in various important ways, the LDS at the beginning of the twentieth century had bowed to Protestant norms about church–state separation that they had resisted for several decades.

As part of that process, the LDS shifted their understanding of what it meant to build God's kingdom on earth. Instead of gathering to Utah to create an LDS state, converts outside Utah were encouraged to build the kingdom in their home communities, meaning to build up congregations. LDS envisioned that at some point in the future – at Jesus's second coming – their kingdom would once again take on political and economic aspects. But for the foreseeable future, their church would be a *religious* community only.

State supremacy: An even more pressing problem for the LDS during the late 1800s – more pressing than the issue of church–state separation – was their resistance to state supremacy. That resistance centered on polygamy, although non-state-sanctioned violence was also an issue.

The first U.S. officials sent to govern Utah during the 1850s sensed quickly that the LDS resented their presence and had little respect for their authority. Out of an exaggerated fear that the LDS might revolt against U.S. rule, federal troops marched to Utah in 1857–1858, sparking an exaggerated fear on the part of the LDS that they were in danger of extermination, as in Missouri. After the LDS used guerilla warfare tactics to harass the federal troops, a peaceful resolution was negotiated. Before that peaceful resolution, though, LDS militiamen in southern Utah committed an atrocity. Partly as revenge for what Mormons had suffered in Missouri, the militiamen massacred a party of emigrants – over 120 men, women, and children – who were on their way to California. The Mountain Meadows Massacre, as it is known, together with an attempted cover-up by LDS leaders, fed the public image of Mormonism as a dangerous, lawless religion. However, the 1857–1858 war and the Mountain Meadows Massacre marked the end of violent LDS resistance to state authority. From that point forward, LDS resistance to the state was nonviolent.

Over the second half of the 1800s, the U.S. government waged an increasingly intense campaign to force LDS to submit to laws against polygamy. We'll discuss Mormon polygamy in greater detail in chapter 4. For now, what is important to know is that the LDS regarded polygamy as something that God had commanded their community to practice. Forced to choose between obeying the state's law and God's law, the LDS chose God's law. Hundreds of polygamous LDS men were sent to prison; thousands of LDS fled to Canada and Mexico to keep their polygamous families together; church leaders went into hiding to avoid arrest. Laws were passed to strip LDS of the right to vote, and eventually Congress revoked the LDS Church's legal recognition, authorizing the government to confiscate the church's property.

The LDS took the government to court, arguing that the anti-polygamy campaign violated their constitutional right to free exercise of religion. In a landmark 1879 case called *Reynolds v. United States* (named for George Reynolds, an LDS polygamist), the Supreme Court ruled for the first time in U.S. history on the meaning of the First Amendment's guarantee of religious freedom. The Court ruled that the First Amendment guaranteed citizens freedom of belief, but it did not guarantee them the freedom to act on their beliefs. If people could claim to be exempt from laws that conflicted with their religion, the Court argued, then the authority of the state would be meaningless. The LDS were free to *believe* in polygamy; but because the state had declared polygamy illegal, the LDS were not free to *practice* it, the First Amendment notwithstanding.

REYNOLDS V. UNITED STATES

In 1879, the U.S. Supreme Court ruled against George Reynolds, an LDS polygamist who argued that the federal law against polygamy violated his First Amendment right to the free exercise of religion. This landmark ruling continues to shape the way the courts interpret – more precisely, the way the courts limit – the Constitution's promise of religious freedom.

Congress cannot pass a law [according to the First Amendment] which shall prohibit the free exercise of religion. . . . The question to be determined is, whether the law now under consideration comes within this prohibition. . . .

Polygamy has always been odious among the northern and western nations of Europe, and, until the establishment of the Mormon Church, was almost exclusively a feature of the life of Asiatic and of African people. . . . . [I]t is impossible to believe that the constitutional guaranty of religious freedom was intended to prohibit legislation in respect to this most important feature of social life. Marriage, while from its very nature a sacred obligation, is nevertheless, in most civilized nations, a civil contract, and usually regulated by law. . . .

In our opinion, the statute immediately under consideration is within the legislative power of Congress. . . . This being so, the only question which remains is, whether those who make polygamy a part of their religion are excepted from the operation of the statute. If they are, then those who do not make polygamy a part of their religious belief may be found guilty and punished, while those who do, must be acquitted and go free. This would be introducing a new element into criminal law. Laws are made for the government of actions, and while they cannot interfere with mere religious belief and opinions, they may with practices. . . .

Can a man excuse [actions contrary to the law] because of his religious belief? To permit this would be to make the professed doctrines of religious belief superior to the law of the land, and in effect to permit every citizen to become a law unto himself. Government could exist only in name under such circumstances.

Source: *Reynolds v. United States*, 98 U.S. 145 (1878).

Although the LDS denounced the Court's ruling as unjust, once the Supreme Court had ruled against them, their only options were either to submit to the state or to persist in a resistance that appeared to be leading to their movement's destruction. A way out of the dilemma opened up in 1890, when church president Wilford Woodruff announced that he had received a revelation from God instructing the LDS to submit to the law so that the church would survive. No longer would the LDS have to choose between obeying God and obeying the state – those were now the same thing. Six years after Woodruff's announcement renouncing polygamy, Utah became a state. The LDS had persuaded the federal government that they accepted its supremacy. Their submission was not altogether genuine at first: church leaders privately permitted polygamy even after Woodruff's 1890 announcement. But from about 1905 on, the LDS Church was committed to halting new polygamous marriages.

FUNDAMENTALISTS AND THE STATE

Not all LDS, however, accepted their leaders' submission to the state. The Fundamentalists who gathered around Loren C. Woolley were convinced that God's commandment to practice polygamy remained in force: for them, the state was still in opposition to God. Fundamentalists also rejected some of the accommodations that the LDS made with Protestant ideals of church–state separation. Fundamentalist communities continued to aspire to theocratic ideals, and continued to clash with the state because of it.

Church–state separation: Many, though by no means all, Fundamentalists have gathered into their own communities, located mostly in the western United States, Canada, and Mexico. The most well-known Fundamentalist communities are Hildale/Colorado City, which straddles the Utah-Arizona border, and the (now defunct) Yearning for Zion Ranch in Texas. Both of those communities are associated with the FLDS Church. As the LDS had attempted to do in the 1800s, the FLDS set out to create their own church-run economy, which resulted in the church owning most of the property and housing in Hildale/Colorado City. This arrangement gave Warren Jeffs, who led the FLDS in the early 2000s, the power to expel dissident FLDS from their homes – homes they had constructed but that the church owned. A number of church–state controversies developed around the FLDS in Hildale/Colorado City after Jeffs became their leader. FLDS in positions of local government were accused of misusing state funds or discriminating against ex-FLDS or non-FLDS residents. The state of Utah intervened, reducing the economic power of the FLDS by taking over the organization that administered the FLDS Church's financial holdings – much as the federal government had moved to take over the LDS Church's property during the late 1800s. Ironically, the Utah state officials who conceived and carried out this early twenty-first century action against the FLDS were LDS.

We've seen that nineteenth-century Americans perceived Mormonism as tyrannical because Mormons allowed religious authority to govern their lives in ways that Protestants regarded as intrusive. Americans in the late twentieth and early twenty-first centuries had similar perceptions about Fundamentalists, often expressed as concern that Fundamentalist communities are "cults." Much of the concern has centered on allegations of underage girls being forced into polygamous relationships. There is a parallel here to the 1800s, when anti-polygamists alleged that Mormons were coercing or tricking women into polygamous marriages. Both in the 1800s and now, some former polygamous wives have described their marriages as pressured or abusive; other polygamous women have insisted that their marriages are consensual. There have also been reports of teenage boys being expelled from FLDS communities to fend for themselves, ostensibly to reduce competition for plural wives. Controversies surrounding authoritarian FLDS leader Warren Jeffs, who ended up on the FBI's Ten Most Wanted list, have bolstered perceptions of polygamous Mormon communities as cultish.

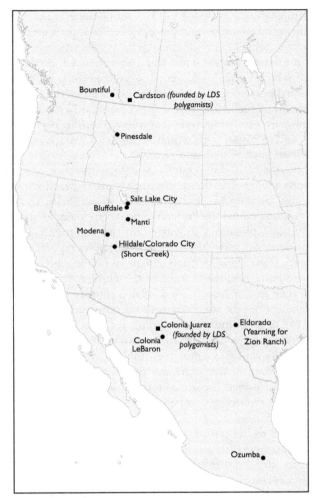

Figure 3.1 Mormon polygamy in western North America. Round dots indicate communities with significant Fundamentalist populations. Note the proximity of Fundamentalist communities in Canada and Mexico to communities founded in the late 1800s by LDS polygamists fleeing the United States, indicated by square markers.

Adapted from Cardell K. Jacobson and Lara Burton, eds., *Modern Polygamy in the United States: Historical, Cultural, and Legal Issues* (New York: Oxford University Press, 2011), xvi. Adaptation courtesy of John Hamer.

Fundamentalists outside the FLDS Church, such as the AUB, have been concerned to dispel such perceptions about their own communities, hence non-FLDS Fundamentalists' participation in the reality television programs *Sister Wives* and *Polygamy USA*, or the enthusiasm with which some Fundamentalists greeted the positive portrayal of a fictional polygamous family in the HBO series *Big Love*. In these programs, Fundamentalists appear as people who have willingly chosen an unconventional lifestyle that allows them to be true to their beliefs – and to values with which mainstream Americans can relate at some level, such as faith and family.

State supremacy: Clearly, Fundamentalists have not accepted the state's authority to tell them that they cannot practice polygamy. Periodically, the state has moved to assert its authority. In 1953, the state of Arizona raided the Fundamentalist settlement at Short Creek (now Hildale/Colorado City), arresting the community's men and taking custody of their children. However, news reports of children being torn from their mothers led to a public opinion backlash against the state. Eventually most of the families were reunited and resumed their lives in Short Creek. Half a century later, in 2008, history seemed to repeat itself when Texas state authorities raided the satellite FLDS community at Yearning for Zion Ranch, again taking the community's children into custody. Again the state's action provoked criticism, and again the children were returned to their parents. However, in the aftermath of the raid, a number of FLDS men were imprisoned for sexual relationships with minors. Warren Jeffs had been arrested a year before the raid, also on charges related to sex with minors.

By contrast to the campaign against LDS polygamy in the 1800s, today's Fundamentalists are not prosecuted for polygamy per se. In the century since the campaign against LDS polygamy, American society has become more tolerant of unconventional sexual arrangements among consenting adults. The state pursues Fundamentalists for other reasons, notably for relationships with minors. Some Fundamentalists have tried to preserve marriage patterns from the 1800s, when it was more acceptable than now for a girl to marry in her teens. Today, however, the state will not permit that. Fundamentalists have therefore had to give up that practice – under duress in the case of the FLDS, although other Fundamentalist groups, such as the AUB, have rejected underage marriages willingly and emphatically.

Welfare fraud is another reason for which the state has prosecuted Fundamentalists: some Fundamentalist families secure welfare benefits by claiming that the wives are single mothers. Reportedly, Fundamentalists defend this fraud on the grounds that they are justified in taking advantage of the state, given the state's persecution of them.

Occasionally Fundamentalists have violated the state's monopoly on violence, drawing on teachings from Brigham Young about blood atonement. For instance, there have been allegations of Fundamentalist men whipping their wives or children to punish them for their sins. During the 1970s, Ervil LeBaron, the leader of a very small Fundamentalist group, instructed his followers that God had commanded them to kill members of other Fundamentalist groups. At least twenty-five murders were carried out at LeBaron's orders; he was eventually imprisoned. Another infamous case of Fundamentalist violence occurred during the 1980s, when two brothers, Ron and Dan Lafferty, murdered their sister-in-law Brenda, together with her baby, because they blamed her for persuading Ron's wife not to agree to let him take a polygamous wife. Most Fundamentalists, we should emphasize, have not engaged in such violence. Like the LDS after the 1850s, the Fundamentalists' strategies in dealing with the state have usually been to quietly evade the law, to seek redress through the courts, or to sway public opinion in their favor.

LDS POLITICAL INVOLVEMENT IN THE TWENTIETH AND TWENTY-FIRST CENTURIES

Of the three major Mormon streams, the LDS have been the most influential in American politics. The large numbers of LDS concentrated in Utah and other western states make them a significant voting force. The Reorganization has been much less significant politically because it doesn't have the same concentrated numbers anywhere in the country. For example, during the entire twentieth century, only one RLDS served as a U.S. senator (a Republican from North Dakota) while another served in the House of Representatives (a Democrat from Iowa). A few RLDS individuals have served in prominent unelected positions, including a U.S. ambassador and a White House press secretary. The Fundamentalists have very little political influence outside their own communities, such as Hildale/

Colorado City, both because they are so few and because of their problematic relationship to the law.

By contrast, dozens of LDS politicians served in high-level elected office in the United States during the twentieth and early twenty-first centuries: as state governors, Congressional representatives, and senators. Two individuals even held federal office at the same time they were serving as apostles, one of the very highest offices in the LDS Church. The first of these was Reed Smoot, who in 1903 was chosen by the Utah state legislature to serve as a senator in Washington D.C. The fact that Smoot was also an apostle provoked opposition from American Protestants who saw Smoot's election as a sign that the LDS still aspired to theocratic power. After three years of hearings, the Senate decided to let Smoot keep his seat – an important sign that Americans were becoming satisfied that the LDS indeed recognized state supremacy and church–state separation. Smoot served as Utah's senator for thirty years. During the 1950s, Dwight Eisenhower appointed another LDS apostle, Ezra Taft Benson, to serve on his presidential cabinet as Secretary of Agriculture. This time, the presence of a high-ranking LDS church leader in a high-ranking government position did not spark significant protests.

When the LDS Church dissolved its political party at the end of the 1800s, LDS voters moved into the Republican and Democratic parties. (There are stories about LDS leaders at the time dividing congregations down the middle, instructing one side of the room to register as Republican and the other side as Democrat. If true, these stories are ironic since LDS leaders were trying to assure the country that they didn't direct their members' voting.) However, as the twentieth century progressed, the LDS vote became much more solidly Republican. This was part of a larger shift that occurred in American politics after the 1960s. The 1960s saw many Americans embrace liberalized values around gender and sexuality; this liberalization led to, among other things, the legalization of abortion and the beginning of the gay rights movement. In reaction to these developments, many religious conservatives were attracted to the Republican Party, which positioned itself as the pro-life party and the party of traditional family values. Those values resonated with many evangelical Protestants, many Catholics – and many LDS. Religious conservatives after the 1960s were also troubled by increasing secularism in American society, such as court rulings restricting prayer in public schools or removing religious symbols like the Ten Commandments from government spaces. Protesting that the principle of church–state separation had been distorted into government hostility against religion, religious conservatives called for a return of religious values to government. Many LDS shared these concerns about secularism. LDS politician Mitt Romney voiced those concerns when he ran for U.S. president in 2008 and 2012.

Some LDS embraced far-right politics at the edges of the U.S. political mainstream if not outside it. A high-profile example is radio host and one-time Fox News television personality Glenn Beck. A convert to the LDS Church, Beck espoused a right-wing libertarianism, according to which the U.S. Constitution's protections for individual rights were under attack from a conspiracy of progressives in business and government. Beck drew on writings of arch-conservative LDS ideologues from the 1960s, whose writings contained echoes, in turn, of nineteenth-century LDS leaders who had denounced the anti-polygamy Raid as a tyrannical government assault on divinely inspired constitutional rights. This constitutionalist, anti-government strain among the LDS found a more dramatic manifestation in the Bundy family of Nevada, who in 2014 and 2016 engaged in armed standoffs with federal agents whose authority the Bundys considered illegitimate. Some LDS sympathized with Beck's or the Bundys' hard-right views; others were embarrassed or appalled.

While most LDS in the United States stood somewhere along the political right, a small minority espoused liberal or even socialist ideologies, which they saw as aligned with LDS teachings about helping the poor and other vulnerable minorities. Harry Reid, a Democrat and LDS convert, served for eight years as the Senate majority leader during the early 2000s.

The early twenty-first century saw both a high point and a low point for LDS participation in American politics. The high point came during the 2012 election, when Republicans chose Mitt Romney to be their presidential candidate. Romney's candidacy was a sign of how far the LDS had come in gaining acceptance within the mainstream of American society. It also showed how much the American political landscape had changed over the course of a century. At the beginning of the twentieth century, many American Protestants – many of them Republican – still suspected that the LDS did not really support church–state separation and had not really given up their commitment to polygamy. At the beginning of the twenty-first century, Republicans – many of them Protestant – rallied around an LDS presidential candidate who called for a greater role for religion in government and a defense of "traditional marriage." Indeed, much had changed!

Four years earlier, however, in 2008, American LDS experienced a political low when church leadership decided to support Proposition 8, a California ballot initiative barring gay marriage. Church leaders urged LDS to donate money and time to the campaign for Proposition 8 and helped organize them to do so. After a close race, the proposition passed – at which point the LDS found themselves the target of an angry backlash, expressed in protests outside LDS temples in California and Utah and calls for boycotts of businesses with LDS owners. Critics accused the church of inappropriately meddling in politics; LDS who had not supported Proposition 8 reported feeling pressured or intimidated by church leaders. These criticisms of the LDS Church echoed criticisms of Mormon theocracy made during the 1800s. On the other hand, LDS supporters of Proposition 8 objected to what they saw as attempts to deny their right to participate in the democratic process; some LDS compared the backlash to the persecution LDS had faced in the 1800s. If Mitt Romney's presidential candidacy showed how much things had changed from the 1800s, the controversy around Proposition 8 suggested that in other ways, the LDS relationship with the state remained problematic.

A GLANCE AT MORMONS AND THE STATE OUTSIDE THE UNITED STATES

Although Mormons have enjoyed the greatest political prominence in the United States, LDS individuals have also been elected to national legislatures in a few British Commonwealth nations (Britain, Canada, and New Zealand) and in Latin America (Mexico and Brazil). As Mitt Romney ran unsuccessfully for U.S. president in 2012, an LDS convert named Yeah Samake ran unsuccessfully for the presidency of Mali. Some Mormons in the Reorganization stream have served in national legislatures in Canada and French Polynesia.

In contrast to LDS defiance of American anti-polygamy laws during the 1800s, subsequent LDS leaders have urged members to dutifully obey the governments under which they live, even repressive governments. This policy allowed German LDS trapped behind the Iron Curtain to win sufficient trust from East Germany's socialist government that the church was allowed to construct a temple there – this despite the anti-Communist preaching of some American LDS leaders. But the policy of obedience to governments could also put the LDS on the wrong side of history, as when Helmuth Hübener, an LDS 17-year-old in Nazi Germany, was excommunicated from the church for writing tracts opposing Nazism. (After World War II ended – and after the Nazis had beheaded him – Hübener was memorialized among LDS for his heroism.)

Sometimes governments have restricted the LDS. Ghana, for instance, expelled missionaries and ordered churches closed for a time at the end of the 1980s because the government perceived the LDS Church as promoting disloyalty to the state (perhaps due to the church's American ties). In some such cases, LDS politicians in the United States have been able to use their influence to help protect their coreligionists elsewhere in the world. In the mid-1990s, Orrin Hatch, an LDS senator representing Utah, persuaded other U.S. senators to join him in lodging a formal protest with the Russian government after an official there denounced the LDS as a cult who threatened Russia's security.

Both the LDS and the Reorganization have at times been associated, willingly or unwillingly, with U.S. imperialism. The most notable instance of this in the Reorganization occurred in the 1890s, when the United States annexed Hawaii following an American-led coup that toppled the native government. A prominent RLDS pastor, a white American, allowed the U.S. Marines to use a church building in Hawaii as their headquarters, thereby alienating many of the Reorganization's native Hawaiian converts. In South America during the 1980s, Marxist militants fire-bombed LDS chapels and murdered some LDS missionaries, perceiving them as proxies for the U.S. government, which supported the authoritarian regimes that the militants aimed to bring down.

In some places, members of the Reorganization have faced violent persecution. During the 1850s, Tahitian Mormons, most of whom eventually became RLDS, were forbidden to worship by the Catholic-aligned French colonial government; when authorities tried to shut down one Mormon worship service, a lethal scuffle resulted in several Tahitian converts, women and men, being sentenced to a chain gang. In the early 2000s, some Community of Christ members in India were caught up in anti-Christian violence perpetrated by militant Hindu nationalists.

Surprisingly, perhaps, Fundamentalists in Mexico and Canada have had few confrontations with their governments. The most dramatic exception is when Mexican authorities arrested Ervil LeBaron for a murder he ordered there. Fundamentalist colonies outside the United States have not experienced state opposition as intense as the raids in Short Creek and Eldorado.

CONCLUSION

We end this chapter with a coda to the story with which we began: the raid on the FLDS community at Yearning for Zion Ranch in Eldorado. In April 2014, six years after the raid, the Texas government received permission from the courts to seize ownership of the ranch on the grounds that it had been used for a criminal purpose – sex with minors. After state officials informed them of the impending legal action, the last few residents who had not already abandoned the ranch following the raid did so. Thus ended the FLDS presence in this rural Texas community. The state had decisively wielded its authority to ensure that its laws would be obeyed above any deeply held religious commitments to the contrary.

Dominant American concepts of church–state relations grew out of the experience of English Protestants in the colonial era. The basic principles emerging from this experience were two-fold: state supremacy and church–state separation. These principles set limits on what counts in the United States as religious freedom. While it may seem common sense – as it did to the Supreme Court in the landmark *Reynolds* case – that there need to be limits to religious freedom in American society, where those limits should be remains a disputed question. Mormonism is one of many instances of a religious minority having to accept what some members of the minority perceive as restrictions on their religious freedom in order to submit to dominant notions, Protestant in origin, about proper church–state relations. The different Mormon streams followed different pathways: the Reorganization submitting most quickly to the dominant notions; the LDS resisting but ultimately adapting; the Fundamentalists continuing to resist.

NOTES

1 Amy Joi O'Donoghue, "This Won't Be Another'Short Creek'," *Deseret News,* April 28, 2008.
2 ABC News, *Good Morning America* with Robin Roberts, "Polygamist Mothers Plea: One-On-One Interview Inside Compound," April 17, 2008.
3 Michelle Roberts, "Sweep of Polygamists' Kids Raises Legal Questions," *USA Today*, April 26, 2008.
4 Josiah Strong, *Our Country: Its Possible Future and Its Present Crisis* (New York: American Home Missionary Society, 1885), 61.

SUGGESTIONS FOR FURTHER READING

Randall Balmer and Jana Riess, eds., *Mormonism and American Politics* (New York: Columbia University Press, 2015).

Sarah Barringer Gordon, *The Mormon Question: Polygamy and Constitutional Conflict in Nineteenth-Century America* (Chapel Hill: University of North Carolina Press, 2002).

Kathleen Flake, *The Politics of American Religious Identity: The Seating of Senator Reed Smoot, Mormon Apostle* (Chapel Hill: University of North Carolina Press, 2004).

Patrick Q. Mason, "God and the People: Theodemocracy in Nineteenth-Century Mormonism," *Journal of Church and State* 53, no. 3 (2011): 349–375.

Christine Talbot, *A Foreign Kingdom: Mormons and Polygamy in American Political Culture, 1852–1890* (Urbana: University of Illinois Press, 2013).

Stuart A. Wright and James T. Richardson, eds., *Saints under Siege: The Texas State Raid on the Fundamentalist Latter Day Saints* (New York: New York University Press, 2011).

4

MORMONS AND SEX

GENDER, SEXUALITY, AND FAMILY

Eri grew up as a boy named Eddie in an LDS family in Utah. From a very early age, Eddie felt frustrated with his gender identity. His father recalls that when Eddie was about four years old, he came to him crying, "Daddy, I want to be a girl." By age 16, Eddie, who had been ordained to the LDS priesthood, concluded that he was gay. That decision led to him dropping out of the private LDS high school he attended, at which point he was sent by his parents to spend time with relatives in Japan. There his non-LDS Japanese grandmother suggested, without judgment, that Eddie was not gay but transgender. Returning to the United States with this new understanding of his identity, Eddie persuaded his parents to let him receive hormone replacement therapy and eventually gender reassignment surgery, to transition from male to female – from Eddie to Eri. In a documentary about Eri's experience, *Transmormon,* Eri's father expressed his view that "marriage is between a man and a woman. In my opinion, Eri is a woman. . . . I'm hoping that the leaders of the [LDS] church are going to see it that way, and that she'll be able to get married [in the temple]." In fact, LDS leaders maintain that gender is an eternal trait, and they therefore regard individuals who try to change gender as living contrary to God's plan. As of 2014, Eri had stopped attending church with her parents. As she moved forward with her new gender identity, she was uncertain what would become of her LDS identity.

Eri's personal struggle within Mormonism reflects larger struggles within American culture. Questions around gender and sexuality are among the most contested religious issues in the United States today. Such controversies have been especially intense since the 1960s: think of ongoing controversies about "radical feminists," abortion, contraception, or gay rights. But these kinds of controversies can be traced back much earlier in U.S. history. During the colonial era, Spanish missionaries in the Southwest disapproved of abortion and sexual freedom among Native Americans, while the Puritans in Massachusetts famously banished Anne Hutchinson because she claimed religious authority to teach, a role that Puritan authorities considered improper for a woman. During the 1800s, American Jews split into multiple denominations over whether men and women could be seated together during worship (among other issues); some Christian denominations courted controversy by licensing women as preachers or ordaining them as ministers; and Americans debated whether or not God intended that women should have the vote. Also during that century, white American Protestants expressed alarm about the alleged sexual immorality of various minority groups, including Native Americans, African Americans, Asian immigrants, Catholic priests – and Mormon polygamists.

From Mormonism's first decades down to the present, norms about gender and sexuality have been a useful measure of where Mormons stand in relation to dominant trends in American culture. During the 1800s, polygamy was *the* central issue defining Mormons' place in American culture: the fact that the LDS practiced it attracted fierce opposition, while the Reorganization was emphatic about disavowing it. Once the LDS abandoned polygamy, LDS and Reorganization teachings about gender and sexuality were quite similar – until the 1960s, when the two parted ways again along a liberal-conservative divide that ran through the entire American religious landscape during that period, with the Reorganization on the liberal side and the LDS on the conservative. The Fundamentalists, meanwhile, have remained on the margins of American society because of their very conservative views on gender and their radical insistence on retaining polygamy – although with some signs of growing acceptance in an era more tolerant of sexual minorities.

In this chapter, you'll read about:

- Sex, family, and gender in early Mormonism.
- Mormon polygamy: past, present . . . and future?
- Gender roles and "family values" in contemporary Mormonism.
- Teachings about homosexuality in the Mormon streams.

SEX, FAMILY, AND GENDER IN EARLY MORMONISM

The Book of Mormon gave little hint – although it did give some – of the unconventional directions that Mormonism would take during the last years of Joseph Smith Jr.'s leadership. Polygamy was discussed in one passage, where it was *condemned* as an abomination that caused anguish to the tender hearts of women. The same passage did say, however, that polygamy was lawful if God commanded it – suggesting, perhaps, that Smith was already contemplating the possibility of such a command. Otherwise, the Book of Mormon's teachings on sexual morality were conventionally conservative: deny your lusts, do not fornicate, do not commit adultery. As for gender, men dominated the Book of Mormon. Women barely appeared in the book, and when they did they were usually in the background, rarely major actors. The Book of Mormon's world was literally patriarchal: much emphasis was placed on the leadership of fathers passing to sons.

Like its founding scripture, early Mormonism was male-dominated. The many priesthood offices that developed within Mormonism were held exclusively by men. Most of the revelations compiled in Doctrine and Covenants were delivered to men, either as individuals or as members of priesthood councils. A number of individual men were chastised in the revelations for not properly governing their households or rearing their children – an expression of patriarchal values. The revelations contained no instructions specifically for women about child-rearing. That omission is striking given that during this same period of history, American culture was coming to give women a more central place in the home: as mothers, they were responsible for the moral and religious upbringing of their children, while as wives, they were responsible for making the home a sanctuary from the rough-and-tumble values of the increasingly industrialized, capitalist world in which their husbands struggled to make a living. Mormon scripture had comparatively little to say to women along these lines; it spoke more about the spiritual leadership of fathers. In this regard, early Mormonism was more conservative – more patriarchal – than nineteenth-century American culture on the whole.

During Mormonism's Nauvoo era, family took on special significance in Joseph Smith Jr.'s teachings, and as a result, women took on new roles in the movement. A women's organization was created, the Relief Society, inspired by similar organizations among Protestant women that provided aid to the poor. The initiative to create the Relief Society came from Mormon women, not by a revelation from Smith, although Smith immediately took over the idea when the women presented it to him. Smith said he would make the Relief Society a "kingdom of priests" – striking language in a movement where priesthood had up to this point been exclusively male. Exactly what Smith meant by that expression remains debated among Mormons to the present.

The formation of the Relief Society was the most publicly visible development for women during the Nauvoo period. Other developments occurred secretly – or were meant to have stayed secret. Smith formed a secret inner circle of men and women, husbands and wives, who inaugurated new rites that would eventually be performed in the Nauvoo Temple, an edifice not completed during Smith's lifetime. The new rituals included marriage (or sealing) for all eternity, as well as rites of anointing that prepared couples to exercise divine power in the afterlife. Participants in these rites, women as well as men, wore biblical-style robes that symbolized priestly office. Men were anointed to become kings and priests to God; women were anointed to become queens and priestesses to their husbands.

The new rites were connected to a secretly circulating revelation written by Smith, which the LDS later published as Doctrine and Covenants 132. The revelation taught that men and women whose marriages were sealed for eternity would be exalted to the status of Gods in the world to come, with the ability to go on producing posterity forever. This same revelation authorized Smith to perform plural marriages, uniting one man with multiple women; as biblical precedent, the revelation cited the polygamous marriages of Abraham, Jacob, Moses, and David. Thus, a patriarchal, polygamous conception of the family was integrated into a Mormon vision of heaven: exalted men surrounded by polygamous wives and an eternally expanding circle of children, grandchildren, great-grandchildren, etc.

The teaching that married couples could become Gods gave rise to a corollary, which Smith reportedly taught to one of his plural wives, Eliza R. Snow. Snow expressed the new doctrine in a poem that became a popular LDS hymn: "In the heavens are parents single? / No, the thought makes reason stare! / Truth is reason, truth eternal / tells me I've a mother there." In other words: God, who fathered our immortal spirits before the world began, has a wife, our Heavenly Mother. Later in the 1800s, LDS teachers who regarded polygamy as essential to attaining Godhood theorized, by extension, that God is a polygamist, which would mean that there are multiple Heavenly Mothers.

DOCTRINE AND COVENANTS 132 (EXCERPTS)

The LDS and the Fundamentalists accept this document as the revelation in which God commanded Joseph Smith Jr. to reinstitute the biblical practice of polygamy. Until the late twentieth century, the RLDS took the position that the document is a fraud, meaning they denied that Smith wrote it; but its authenticity is not in question among professional historians.

Verily, thus saith the Lord unto you my servant Joseph, that inasmuch as you have inquired of my hand to know and understand wherein I, the Lord, justified my servants Abraham, Isaac, and Jacob, as also Moses, David and Solomon, my servants, as touching the principle and doctrine of their having many wives and concubines –

Behold and lo, I am the Lord thy God and will answer thee as touching this matter.

Therefore, prepare thy heart to receive and obey the instructions which I am about to give unto you; for all those who have this law revealed unto them must obey the same. . . .

God commanded Abraham, and Sarah gave Hagar to Abraham to wife. And why did she do it? Because this was the law; and from Hagar sprang many people. This, therefore, was fulfilling, among other things, the promises.

> Was Abraham, therefore, under condemnation? Verily I say unto you, Nay; for I, the Lord, commanded it. . . .
> Abraham received concubines, and they bore him children; and it was accounted unto him for righteousness, because they were given unto him, and he abode in my law; as Isaac also and Jacob . . . ; and because they did none other things than that which they were commanded, they have entered into their exaltation, according to the promises, and sit upon thrones, and are not angels but are gods.

Source: Doctrine and Covenants 132:1–3, 34–35, 37 (LDS editions).

MORMON POLYGAMY: PAST, PRESENT . . . AND FUTURE?

Rumors about polygamy in Nauvoo fueled outside opposition to Mormonism as well as triggering high-profile defections by Mormon leaders. Following Smith's death, the LDS – whose leaders had belonged to the secret inner circle at Nauvoo – continued to embrace Smith's vision of eternal marriage and Godhood, including polygamy. The Reorganization, by contrast, rejected polygamy as a corruption of their religion, for which they held LDS leaders entirely responsible. Joseph Smith Jr., the Reorganization insisted, had never taught polygamy or practiced it – a denial facilitated by the fact that Smith had publicly condemned polygamy. Through the rest of the 1800s, Reorganization members were preoccupied with making sure that the public understood *they* were not polygamists.

The LDS began practicing polygamy openly once they had settled in the Intermountain West. LDS leaders taught that polygamy was essential to obtain the highest degree of glory – Godhood – in the afterlife. Polygamy was therefore an essential aspect of Mormonism, as LDS leaders understood it. The more wives a man took, the greater his "kingdom" in the world to come. Church leaders tended to have the greatest number of wives: Brigham Young had married 55 women by the time he died. The vast majority of polygamous LDS families were smaller, however, with just two or three wives. Interestingly, even though LDS leaders taught that polygamy was essential for Godhood, most LDS did not practice it: only about one in four LDS during the 1800s lived in a family that practiced polygamy. This fact would suggest that while LDS were willing to accept polygamy as something practiced by some within their religion, most were not keen to practice it themselves. In sermons, LDS leaders expressed frustration that church members were not living up to their obligations in this regard.

Most Americans could readily understand why men would be attracted to polygamy: that is, Americans understood LDS polygamy as a religious cover for male lust. Americans had a harder time understanding how *women* could consent to such a thing. Outsiders tended to imagine that LDS women must have been tricked or intimidated into becoming plural wives. They were therefore surprised when LDS women staged rallies in defense of polygamy. Although LDS women often described polygamy as extremely difficult, they also spoke of it as something they believed God had called them to do – a sacrifice for their faith. In literature of the day, polygamous LDS women were depicted as broken, browbeaten creatures. Contrary to that stereotype, polygamous LDS women of the 1800s included among their ranks activists for women's suffrage, some of the first LDS women to receive medical training, and some of the first women in American history to serve as legislators. On the other hand, some LDS women were so miserable as polygamous wives that they defected, writing autobiographies or going on lecture tours to denounce what they had become convinced were the evils of the LDS Church, polygamy among them.

Critics in the American mainstream opposed polygamy as degrading and oppressive to women and a moral blot on the nation. They equated Mormon polygamy with polygamy in Africa or the Muslim world, which is to say that they saw polygamy as a barbaric, uncivilized practice, from which women needed to be set free. When the Republican Party formed at the end of the 1850s, it dedicated itself to exterminating what its first party platform called "the twin relics of barbarism": slavery and polygamy. Once the Civil War and the 13th Amendment had abolished the first relic, Republicans set out to abolish the second. The LDS responded to the federal government's three-decades long anti-polygamy campaign by embracing a countercultural position. They defiantly insisted that polygamy was superior to monogamy. If polygamy were to become the social norm,

LDS apologists declared, it would cure social ills such as prostitution and children born out of wedlock. The LDS charged their critics with hypocrisy: how many of the male politicians who denounced polygamy had mistresses? By contrast, the apologists argued, LDS men took responsibility for their multiple women. In short, where critics regarded polygamy as a sign of LDS depravity, the LDS touted it as a sign of their moral superiority.

We saw in chapter 3 how the LDS were finally pressured by the federal government to renounce the practice of polygamy. That change created poignant difficulties for existing polygamous families. The government wasn't demanding only that the LDS refrain from forming *further* polygamous families. It also wanted people who had *already* formed polygamous unions to stop living together, since that would be the crime of cohabitation: living together without being legally married. Critics had always regarded polygamous wives as mistresses and their children as bastards. In effect, LDS polygamous families had to submit to those characterizations and to the stigma that went with them.

Or not. There were those who refused to submit. The Fundamentalists retained into the twentieth century the countercultural position that the LDS had embraced during the nineteenth century. However, the Fundamentalists have escaped a federal anti-polygamy campaign as intensive as their LDS predecessors experienced. In part this is because the Fundamentalists' numbers are small, and because, unlike the LDS, they are politically and economically inconsequential beyond their own communities. Furthermore, prosecuting polygamy per se became problematic after the 1960s. Fundamentalists don't typically commit the crime of bigamy, meaning that they don't try to get married *by the state* to more than one person at the same time; their polygamous sealings are religious ceremonies only. Polygamous Mormons would therefore have to be charged instead with the crime of cohabitation. But unless the government is also going to start prosecuting monogamous couples who cohabitate without being married, it exposes itself to charges of discrimination. On occasions when Fundamentalists have been prosecuted, it's typically for crimes other than the mere fact of polygamy, such as welfare fraud, domestic violence, or sex with minors. This was the case for FLDS prophet Warren Jeffs, who in 2006 was arrested by federal authorities and eventually convicted of aggravated rape, meaning sex with two underage girls, 12 and 15, whom he had taken as polygamous wives. In the absence of crimes other than polygamy, state and federal governments generally leave Fundamentalists alone.

There have been prominent exceptions. We referred in chapter 3 to the 1953 raid by Arizona officials on the Fundamentalist settlement at Short Creek. That was followed in 2008 by the Texas government's raid on the FLDS community near Eldorado. It is noteworthy, though, that the Texas raid was a response to allegations of violence and sex with minors, not an anti-polygamy action strictly speaking.

Despite the strong opposition that underage marriages have attracted – resulting in several FLDS men now serving prison sentences – Fundamentalists have at the same time benefited from the increased sexual tolerance of the post-1960s period. Americans have become more willing to accommodate "alternative lifestyles." Fundamentalists have received sympathetic treatment in the media: the fictional HBO series *Big Love*, the reality TV series *Sister Wives*, the documentary *Polygamy USA*. Following the model of another prominent sexual minority, gay/lesbian people, polygamists are coming out of the closet: speaking out, holding rallies, and going to court to call for the decriminalization of their relationships.

Meanwhile, contemporary LDS are ambivalent about polygamy. They clearly do not like to be associated with polygamy in the public mind. When CNN used the LDS temple in Salt Lake City as a visual backdrop for reporting on the crimes of Warren Jeffs, or when HBO began airing *Big Love*, LDS church officials moved quickly to assert that their church had "nothing whatever to do" with the Fundamentalists. However, the LDS Church has not disavowed the doctrine of polygamy; it has merely suspended the practice – or more precisely, it has suspended the practice of marrying polygamously *in this life*. The church still performs polygamous marriages in the sense that a man who has been sealed eternally to one wife can be sealed eternally to another after his first wife dies, thereby creating a polygamous union in the hereafter. On the other hand, LDS leaders have abandoned the nineteenth-century teaching that polygamy is required for exaltation to Godhood. LDS today vary considerably in their attitudes toward polygamy, from seriously expecting that it might be reinstated in this life if the laws of the land change, to lightly joking about the possibility of it being practiced in the hereafter, to struggling to reconcile themselves to the fact that it was ever practiced. While running for president in 2007, Mitt Romney, the great-grandson of polygamists, told an interviewer, "I can't imagine anything more awful than polygamy." Maybe Romney was exaggerating for the sake of his political image, but there is a significant portion of the LDS population today who would agree with his statement.

Meanwhile, Community of Christ has adopted policies that allow some of its members to practice polygamy. In countries where polygamy is a common cultural practice – such as India or some African nations – converts to Community of Christ may continue living in their polygamous marriages, although they are expected not to contract new polygamous marriages once they join the church. This position reflects Community of Christ's commitment to adapting its message to different cultural contexts, as well as concern for the economic well-being of women and children who might be abandoned by a convert husband. Still, the policy has resulted in the irony that the Reorganization stream of Mormonism, which vociferously opposed polygamy in the 1800s, now has openly polygamous members, while the LDS Church, which suspended polygamy to comply with the law of the land, will not accept polygamous members even in countries where polygamy is now legal.

GENDER ROLES AND "FAMILY VALUES" IN CONTEMPORARY MORMONISM

The Industrial Revolution of the 1800s produced an ideology that defined a woman's place as in the home, while men were responsible for outside-the-home tasks like finding a job or voting. That ideology was challenged by two successive waves of feminism: a first wave, in the late 1800s and early 1900s, that gave women access to higher education and the vote; and a second wave in the 1960s and 1970s, which pushed for further gender equality under the law, in the workforce, and in culture, as well as for what advocates described as women's right to control their own bodies through access to contraception and abortion. Second-wave feminism led to a countermovement of social conservatives who feared that society would be harmed by the erosion of what they called traditional gender roles and family values. These social conservatives often cited religious authority; hence they are referred to as the religious right.

Where do the Mormon streams stand in relation to these shifts in Americans' thinking about gender and family?

The Reorganization aligned itself most quickly, during the 1800s, with dominant American thinking about marriage and the home. By retaining polygamy, the LDS held out longer in favor of an even older kind of patriarchy. However, once the LDS suspended the practice of polygamy, their teachings about gender and family quickly aligned themselves with those of the American mainstream. The LDS talked, like other Americans, about the importance of the home as the bedrock of society, about the importance of sexual morality, and about men's and women's roles in ways that were conventional for the time (men as breadwinners, women as homemakers). During the first half of the twentieth century, the LDS and the RLDS sounded very alike in their teaching about gender and the family – and they sounded very much like most Americans. The LDS did retain from the polygamous era a propensity for larger families than the American norm; in this regard, they resembled American Catholics. The RLDS, in contrast, tended to have smaller families; in this, they resembled American Protestants.

Second-wave feminism and other social transformations of the 1960s produced a fault line that cut across the American religious landscape, dividing members of religious groups into conservatives and liberals regarding questions of sexual morality and gender norms. Some religious groups eventually leaned more heavily toward the liberal side, others toward the conservative side. As part of this larger trend in American society, both the LDS Church and the Reorganization experienced new conflicts around gender roles during the latter part of the twentieth century. In both movements, liberal members favored expanded roles for women in church and society, while conservative members rallied under the banner of traditional family values. There is a difference, though: in the Reorganization, the liberals became the dominant group while among the LDS, the conservatives dominated.

The first major clash among the LDS occurred in the 1970s over the proposed (but unratified) Equal Rights Amendment to the U.S. Constitution, which aimed to ban discrimination by sex. The ERA was opposed by conservative Catholics, evangelicals, and others who feared that it would undermine traditional gender roles, eliminate legal protections granted to women, or lead to same-sex marriage.

The LDS Church took the rare step of adopting an official political position, opposing the ERA and mobilizing members to campaign against it. A nationally prominent LDS *supporter* of the ERA, Sonia Johnson, was excommunicated. The ERA controversy dismayed but also solidified the emerging feminist sensibilities of some LDS, while awakening in many others a sense that traditional gender roles, and therefore the family, were under attack.

That sense prompted LDS leadership to issue in 1995 a document usually referred to as the Proclamation on the Family. The Proclamation champions a version of socially conservative family values. "The family is ordained of God," the document declares. "Marriage between man and woman is essential to His eternal plan." Fathers are said to have a God-given role "to preside over their families in love and righteousness and are responsible to provide the necessities of life and protection for their families," while "mothers are primarily responsible for the nurture of their children." At the same time, the Proclamation uses egalitarian language in stating that "fathers and mothers are obligated to help one another as equal partners."[1] Although large numbers of LDS women work outside the home as a matter of economic necessity, church leaders have expressed a strong preference that families make the financial sacrifices necessary to keep mothers at home with their children. While the Proclamation on the Family has not been canonized as scripture, it holds a high status among LDS, many of whom frame it at home, alongside family photos, to express their commitment to divinely ordained family values.

There is no equivalent to the Proclamation on the Family in Community of Christ, which has not integrated conservative family-values rhetoric into its proclamation of the gospel. Strengthening the family and making families eternal are prominent themes in LDS missionary outreach; not so for Community of Christ. When Community of Christ adopted statements of belief and "Enduring Principles" at the beginning of the twenty-first century, these did not include statements about the importance of the family as the foundation of society or about the God-given roles of husbands and wives, nor have statements along those lines appeared in recent additions to Doctrine and Covenants. Consistent with the liberal orientation of its leadership, Community of Christ does not present "family values," a conservative buzz phrase, as part of Christ's message.

The liberal-conservative split between Community of Christ and the LDS over issues of gender can be seen in other ways as well. One is their divergent practices around referring to God as male. In the wake of second-wave feminism, liberal Christians and Jews became persuaded that because God isn't literally male (since God isn't understood in these traditions as having a body), using only male pronouns or images to refer to God reflects cultural biases privileging men over women. Liberal Christians and Jews therefore began using either feminine or – more commonly – gender-neutral language to refer to God. Community of Christ has followed this trend in sermons, hymns, prayers, and in the most recent sections of Doctrine and Covenants. The LDS have not followed this route. In large part this is because the LDS *do* understand God as literally male, in keeping with Joseph Smith Jr.'s Nauvoo-era teachings about God being an exalted man with a body of flesh and bone. However, the LDS teaching about Heavenly Mother opens up the possibility for referring to God as both male *and* female. At the end of the twentieth century, some LDS began to do this, praying to "Our Heavenly Father and Mother," or "Our Heavenly Parents." Church leaders disapproved this practice on the grounds that it had no scriptural precedent: Jesus prayed only to "Our Father."

Another important split around gender roles is women's ordination. Again in the wake of second-wave feminism, several liberal Christian and Jewish groups began ordaining women as ministers and rabbis. Likewise, in the 1970s and 1980s, some members of the RLDS Church began arguing for women's ordination. Debate around this issue came to an end in 1984, when prophet-president Wallace B. Smith (Joseph Smith Jr.'s great-grandson) announced a revelation authorizing the ordaining of women. Approved by a vote of three-fourths of the World Conference, this revelation was canonized as Doctrine and Covenants 156. However, a sizable minority of the Reorganization's members rejected women's ordination, leading to the emergence of breakaway groups. By the first decades of the twenty-first century, Community of Christ had women serving in ordained office at the highest levels – among the Twelve Apostles and in the First Presidency.

Among the LDS, some voices have been advocating women's ordination since the 1980s. But given the more conservative nature of the LDS community, these advocates are a small – if highly visible – minority. Church leaders have reacted by teaching that God has given men and women "equal but complementary" roles, with priesthood belonging to the male role. At times, church leaders have described the symmetry as: men are called to priesthood, women to motherhood. As recently as 2014, Kate Kelly, the leader of a group calling for women's ordination, was excommunicated, an indication that church leaders consider this issue closed. However, LDS leaders have moved to integrate women more fully into church leadership, short of ordaining them – for instance, by having the leadership of the church's women's organizations meet with priesthood leadership councils at both the local and global levels.

What about the Fundamentalists? On the whole, their teachings about gender most closely preserve patriarchal ideals from the 1800s; but they, too, have been affected by larger trends in American culture. Fundamentalists are more likely than contemporary LDS to echo nineteenth-century LDS teachings about women depending on their husbands for their exaltation. In some Fundamentalist communities, women wear dresses that evoke the pioneer era or hairstyles that evoke the early twentieth century, thus symbolizing their commitment to "traditional" values – more traditional, even, than the LDS. Fundamentalists place a premium on large families and on women's roles as mothers and homemakers. On the other hand, the financial challenges of polygamy may require Fundamentalist women to work outside the home – an arrangement facilitated by the fact that other wives can stay at home rearing the children. A recent TV documentary series, *Polygamy USA*, features a Fundamentalist family where two wives work outside the home, leaving one wife at home with the children.

In the post-1960s environment, Fundamentalists are able to selectively borrow messages both from social conservatives and from liberals to try to legitimize their lives to outsiders. To conservatives, Fundamentalists can point to the premium they place on homemaking, child-rearing, and motherhood to suggest that their polygamous families represent a *magnified* commitment to traditional family values. At the same time, Fundamentalists benefit from the increased tolerance that liberal Americans have for nontraditional families, such as gay/lesbian families. Just as in the 1800s, when LDS women became important voices speaking out in favor of polygamy, so too

Fundamentalist women at the beginning of the twenty-first century served as leading defenders of polygamy, challenging stereotypes
of oppressed Fundamentalist women by characterizing polygamy as
an individual choice that society ought to respect. Then again, also
echoing a pattern of the 1800s, alienated Fundamentalist women
have become prominent critics of polygamy, publishing autobiographies and urging the government to take action against what they
describe as an abusive institution.

Fundamentalists have made important adaptations to changing
American norms around gender and sexuality. The most important,
legally, has been to move away from marrying girls in their younger
teens, a practice that would have been acceptable (if not very common) in the 1800s. Another example of changing Fundamentalist
norms can be seen in the Centennial Park community, a group of
former FLDS who came to reject the leadership of Warren Jeffs.
The FLDS had developed a practice called "placement," in which
the prophet would assign girls or women as wives to men he deemed
most worthy. Naturally, this practice runs hard against majority
assumptions about a woman's right to choose her marriage partner
(although the practice would seem less odd to members of societies
who practice arranged marriages today). Centennial Park redefined
the idea of "placement" to mean that young women would seek their
own personal revelation about who God wanted them to marry – a
practice in line with contemporary American norms about women's
right to control their lives.

Community of Christ   **LDS Church**   **Fundamentalists**

Figure 4.1 Families in the three Mormon streams. According to 2014 data, Mormons have the largest families of any religious group in the United States, with
3–4 children on average; the "Mormons" in that survey were most likely LDS.
Community of Christ is the only one of the three streams that accepts gay/
lesbian families.

Image courtesy of John Hamer.

TEACHINGS ABOUT HOMOSEXUALITY IN THE MORMON STREAMS

Like virtually all religious groups in the United States prior to the 1960s, all three Mormon streams took for granted that homosexuality was immoral and unnatural (although there are cases in the historical record of Mormons treating homosexual individuals among them more or less empathetically). The conservative-liberal divide that cut across American society after the 1960s introduced a split in Americans' attitudes toward homosexuality. Liberals supported progressively greater tolerance for homosexuality, which most scientists had come to regard as a natural variation in human sexuality. Within a relatively short time, the United States shifted from homosexuality being a criminal offense to the Supreme Court ruling that state governments were constitutionally obligated to perform same-sex marriages. Religious liberals reinterpreted scriptural condemnations of homosexuality: for example, by judging those texts to reflect the cultural prejudice of ages past. Religious conservatives, by contrast, maintained that biblical teachings against homosexuality were still authoritative, although they tended to say so in less strident tones than in previous decades. Opposition to homosexual relationships was often tied, for religious conservatives, to belief in differentiated gender roles. If you understand men and women as having fundamentally different roles to play in a marriage, then you will naturally see a marriage of two men or two women as fundamentally flawed.

Community of Christ followed other liberal religious groups in moving toward greater acceptance of gay men and lesbians, as measured especially by the questions of whether the church would ordain gay individuals and whether it would marry gay couples. These were divisive questions in Community of Christ, and the leadership moved slowly on the issue, hoping to avoid a repeat of the splits that occurred in the 1980s over women's ordination. The church's increased awareness of its global identity affected matters as well. While a growing proportion of Community of Christ members in the United States were coming to favor gay ordination and gay marriages, in other regions of the world where Community of Christ members lived, disapproval of homosexuality remained more common. Community of Christ members in some African countries feared that affiliation with a pro-gay church could result in legal or violent suppression. By the 2010s, Community of Christ leaders had brokered what they hoped would be a solution. Prophet-president Stephen Veazey presented a revelation allowing the church to call national and regional conferences that would form their own policies regarding homosexuality. The result was that the United States, Canada, Britain, and Australia all held conferences that overwhelmingly voted to authorize marriage and ordination for gay individuals. Community of Christ members in nations such as India, the Philippines, and Haiti retained policies barring same-sex marriages and gay ordination.

DOCTRINE AND COVENANTS 164 (EXCERPT)

In 2010, Community of Christ prophet-president Stephen Veazey presented the following as a revelation to the church. Citing the principles laid out in this document, Community of Christ members in the United States, Canada, Britain, and Australia later voted to adopt policies supporting same-sex marriage and priesthood ordination for gay individuals.

As revealed in Christ, God, the Creator of all, ultimately is concerned about behaviors and relationships that uphold the worth and giftedness of all people and that protect the most vulnerable. Such relationships are to be rooted in the principles of Christ-like love, mutual respect, responsibility, justice, covenant, and faithfulness, against which there is no law.

If the church more fully will understand and consistently apply these principles, questions arising about responsible human sexuality; gender identities, roles, and relationships; marriage; and other issues may be resolved according to God's divine purposes. Be assured, nothing within these principles condones selfish, irresponsible, promiscuous, degrading, or abusive relationships.

Source: Doctrine and Covenants 164:6a-b (Community of Christ editions). Available at cofchrist.org.

By contrast, the LDS retained a stance of moral disapproval toward homosexuality. In this, the LDS were aligned with other American religious conservatives. However, LDS opposition to homosexuality was based on more than teachings from the Bible; it was also based on Joseph Smith Jr.'s Nauvoo-era teachings about exaltation and eternal families. The patriarchal vision of heaven as a husband and wife (or wives) with their expanding posterity was inherently heterosexual. (Recall that the Reorganization didn't retain these Nauvoo-era teachings, which therefore never figured into Community of Christ's debates about homosexuality.)

Like other religiously conservative groups in post-1960s America, the LDS softened their disapproving rhetoric to avoid accusations of prejudice or bigotry in a cultural climate that was increasingly gay-friendly. In the 1970s, LDS leaders condemned homosexuality as "perversion," "abomination," and "selfish," and they supported experiments at Brigham Young University that used electroshock therapy to try to recondition people with homosexual feelings to have heterosexual ones instead. By the beginning of the twenty-first century, church leaders were more sympathetic and more cautious in their language: they expressed sympathy for those who "struggled" with "same-sex attraction," and they left open the possibility that homosexuality might be an unchangeable condition. But the LDS continued to maintain that individuals ought not to act on homosexual desires, and the church remained a staunch opponent of legalizing same-sex marriage. During the 2000s, the church urged its members to support state campaigns protecting "traditional marriage," especially in California. The campaigns succeeded initially, but at the price of a public backlash, and were ultimately overturned by the Supreme Court. In 2015, a few months after same-sex marriage became legal throughout the United States, the church startled observers – and distressed some of its own members – by implementing a policy that barred children of gay couples from being baptized until the child became a legal adult and renounced belief in same-sex marriage. Internationally, LDS forged alliances with other religious conservatives to push back against gay rights movements in other countries or in United Nations initiatives.

Fundamentalists have been publicly quiet about homosexuality. Probably this reflects their relatively greater isolation from the mainstream of American society and its political debates. Presumably,

Fundamentalists disapprove of homosexuality for the same doctrinal reasons the LDS do. Ironically, however, the legalization of same-sex marriage in the United States might prove a step toward the legalization of polygamy. The arguments that the majority of Supreme Court justices gave to establish a constitutional right for gays and lesbians to marry potentially provide grounds for Fundamentalists (and other polygamists in the United States, such as some Muslims) to argue that the government should give legal recognition to their relationships, too. Whether or not the future holds such a development remains to be seen.

CONCLUSION

Regarding both gender roles and sexual practices, the first Mormons were conventional, even conservative, compared to the dominant American Protestant culture around them. Polygamy, however, introduced in the 1840s, made Mormons stand out radically – not only from the larger society but also from one another. Conflicts within Mormonism over whether to practice polygamy were one of the main factors giving rise to the three Mormon streams we've profiled throughout this book: the Reorganization, who rejected polygamy from the time it was introduced; the LDS, who practiced polygamy until the end of the 1800s; and the Fundamentalists, who kept practicing polygamy after the LDS abandoned it.

In those three Mormon streams today, different practices around gender, sexuality, and the family mirror larger divides in post-1960s American culture. Community of Christ stands on the liberal side of the so-called "culture wars" over gender and sexuality: the church performs same-sex marriages (at least in some nations), ordains women, and generally lacks family-values rhetoric. The LDS stand on the conservative side of this same divide: it rejects same-sex marriage and women's ordination and calls its members to defend the family. Fundamentalists are even more conservative than today's LDS to the extent that Fundamentalist family values remain more unabashedly patriarchal. However, Fundamentalists have benefitted from Americans' growing liberal tolerance of nontraditional family models, at least among consenting adults. As it was in the beginning, so it is still: sex reproduces not only new Mormons, but also new Mormonisms.

NOTE

1 Church of Jesus Christ of Latter-day Saints, "The Family: A Proclamation to the World," September 23, 1995, available at lds.org.

SUGGESTIONS FOR FURTHER READING

Janet Bennion, *Polygamy in Primetime: Gender, Media, and Politics in Mormon Fundamentalism* (Lebanon, NH: University Press of New England, 2012).

Matthew Bowman and Kate Holbrook, eds., *Women and the LDS Church in Historical and Contemporary Perspective* (Salt Lake City: University of Utah Press, 2016).

Joanna Brooks, Rachel Hunt Steenblik, and Hannah Wheelwright, eds., *Mormon Feminism: Essential Writings* (New York: Oxford University Press, 2015).

Richley H. Crapo, "Latter-day Saint Lesbian, Gay, Bisexual, and Transgendered Spirituality," in *Gay Religion*, edited by Scott Thumma and Edward R. Gray (Walnut Creek, CA: AltaMira, 2005), 99–113.

Kathryn M. Daynes, *More Wives Than One: Transformation of the Mormon Marriage System, 1840–1910* (Urbana: University of Illinois Press, 2008).

Danny L. Jorgensen and Joni Wilson, eds., *Herstories: Ten Autobiographical Narratives of RLDS Women* (Independence, MO: John Whitmer Books, 2013).

Rocky O'Donovan, "The Abominable and Detestable Crime against Nature: A Brief History of Homosexuality and Mormonism, 1840–1980," in *Multiply and Replenish: Mormon Essays on Sex and Family*, edited by Brent Corcoran (Salt Lake City: Signature Books, 1994), 123–170.

William D. Russell, ed., *Homosexual Saints: The Community of Christ Experience* (Independence, MO: John Whitmer Books, 2008).

Stephen C. Taysom, "A Uniform and Common Recollection: Joseph Smith's Legacy, Polygamy, and the Creation of Mormon Public Memory, 1852–2002," *Dialogue: A Journal of Mormon Thought* 35, no. 3 (Fall 2002): 113–144.

THE SHAPE OF A MORMON LIFE

RITUAL AND REGULATION

Lindsey and Logan are LDS siblings, two years apart. Lindsey, a first-year college student at Brigham Young University, has decided to submit her "mission papers" – that is, she is applying to serve an 18-month proselytizing mission for the church. She is under no pressure to do so, but she wants to take this time off before she finishes college or gets married, which she is likely to do somewhat younger than most Americans, given LDS norms. Lindsey's younger brother Logan is a junior in high school. Their family takes for granted that Logan will serve a two-year mission once he graduates; his parents have been saving money for that purpose for years. Logan himself has never made a conscious decision to serve, but he accepts missionary service as part of normal life for an LDS male. He looks forward to the experience, positively but somewhat vaguely, much as he looks forward to going to college somewhere, marrying someone, and having children someday. Although Lindsey's parents did not expect her to serve a mission, they are proud of her decision and will use money they saved for her college education to support her as a missionary.

Chris is a young adult in Community of Christ. Like many American young adults, Chris is looking to find out more about herself, and she wants to experience a culture other than her own. She has decided to spend the summer before her sophomore year of college working with Community of Christ's World Service Corps. Her assignment will take her to the Philippines, where she will work with humanitarian NGOs in rural villages. Much like Logan's and Lindsey's missionary experiences, Chris's summer with the World Service Corps will prove life-changing, connecting her more strongly to her church and its values. Chris will not proselytize for Community of Christ in the Philippines, but when she returns home, members of her congregation will notice that she takes her religion more seriously. The congregation's leaders may contemplate inviting her to be ordained to an office in the priesthood.

Lindsey, Logan, and Chris are imaginary, but they represent the real-life experiences of LDS and Community of Christ young adults. We'll refer back to the three of them throughout this chapter to illustrate differences between LDS and Community of Christ patterns for living. The three will also illustrate how the lives of people in the LDS Church and Community of Christ can differ from what many Americans regard as typical. Young adulthood in contemporary America is often a period for exploring new identities. Many middle-class Americans study abroad for a semester in college or take "gap years" to visit other parts of the world or explore career possibilities. Fewer young adults go on multi-year missions for religious organizations or work abroad for a humanitarian NGO for a summer. By contrast, Mormons like Lindsey, Logan, and Chris develop their identities through *rites* and *regulations* they encounter in their respective churches.

Mormonism, like other religious traditions, has developed various means by which individuals create identities, structure their lives, and find meaning in everyday routines. Depending on their tradition, people may do these things by observing holy days, rites of passage and other life-cycle landmarks (such as weddings and funerals), regulations on diet or dress, or other forms of spiritual discipline. Ritualized actions and regulations like these shape how people live as individuals, within a group, and in relation to outsiders. The ways of living adopted by members of a particular religious group can place them in higher or lower tension with other groups in society, depending on how different the groups' ways of living are. "Tension" in this sense does not necessarily imply conflict, although it can; what it certainly implies is "standing out" to a greater or lesser degree from others. A Jew who keeps kosher is in higher tension with the American mainstream than one who does not. The same is true of a Muslim woman who wears a head covering, an evangelical Christian who pledges to abstain from sex before marriage, or a family of Jehovah's Witnesses who do not celebrate Christmas.

The particular ways in which Mormons live place them in higher or lower tension with whatever pass as the cultural norms at a given historical moment. Comparing the three Mormon streams, the general pattern today is that Fundamentalists are in very high tension with mainstream American culture, the LDS are in moderately high tension, and the Reorganization is in less tension. We will illustrate this pattern as we examine the following:

- Ritual in Mormon lives: routines and life cycles.
- Regulation of Mormon lives: diet, dress, discipline, and charisma.

RITUAL IN MORMON LIVES

Early Mormons adopted rites common to other Christian traditions, including baptism (by full immersion underwater, like the Baptists did), the sacrament of the Lord's Supper (partaking of bread and wine, also known as communion), and healing by the laying on of hands (a rite that became common among Pentecostals as well). In addition, Mormons developed unique rites, most notably the Nauvoo-era temple ceremonies. Early Mormons referred to their rites as "ordinances." The LDS continue to use that term today, but Community of Christ has shifted to "sacraments," a term more common in other Christian denominations.

Whether called ordinances or sacraments, these rites play important roles in Mormons' lives. Rites offer a way to confront unusual circumstances or stresses. In all three streams of Mormonism, individuals who are sick may request a health blessing, in which priesthood holders anoint the person with a little olive oil, lay their hands on the person's head, and speak whatever words of comfort or promise they feel that the Holy Spirit is inspiring them to say. During the 1800s, LDS women administered such blessings at times, especially for women preparing for childbirth, but this custom disappeared in the twentieth century, leaving health blessings to be the exclusive prerogative of male priesthood holders. This means that if Lindsey, one of our imaginary LDS, requests a health blessing, it will be administered by men – most likely her father, perhaps assisted by Logan once he has been ordained an elder. If Chris requests a health blessing, the priesthood holders who administer it could be either men or women, since Community of Christ has been ordaining women to the priesthood since the 1980s.

RITUAL AND ROUTINE

Rites are not just for unusual circumstances, such as illness: rites are observed routinely as well. Not all of these rites have the status of ordinance or sacrament, but they are religious traditions that create distinctively Mormon ways of organizing or marking the passage of time – daily, weekly, monthly, or yearly.

Daily: Lindsey, Logan, and Chris have all been raised to believe that they ought to spend time every day studying the scriptures. (Whether they actually do it is another question, of course.) For Lindsey and Logan, that might mean waking up early to read from one of the standard works: the Bible, the Book of Mormon, Doctrine and Covenants, or Pearl of Great Price. Chris will almost certainly read from the Bible. Lindsey, Logan, and Chris all grew up being taught to pray individually every morning and evening, as well as praying with their families mornings, evenings, and before meals.

Weekly or monthly: When Lindsey and Logan were growing up, their parents tried to set aside each Monday for "family home evening," a custom that LDS church leaders have promoted since the early twentieth century. Sometimes Lindsey and Logan's parents used this evening to teach a religious lesson to the children; other evenings were dedicated to a recreational activity. Either way, family home evening was a chance for Lindsey and Logan's parents to regularly focus on the sacred task of strengthening their family for time and eternity. Lindsey and Logan plan to continue the tradition when they have their own families.

Sunday worship is a weekly rite among Mormons in all three streams, although with some differences. Lindsey and Logan's LDS congregation performs every Sunday the sacrament of the Lord's supper, when worshippers eat small pieces of bread and drink tiny cups of water in remembrance of Jesus's body and blood. In Chris's Community of Christ congregation, that sacrament is observed once a month, using tiny cups of grape juice instead of water.

On one Sunday a month, all LDS fast (refrain from food and drink) for 24 hours as an act of spiritual discipline. On this Sunday, Lindsey and Logan's family make a special "fast offering" to financially support the church's program to provide for members in need. As a member of Community of Christ, Chris doesn't have the custom of fasting. But her congregation does collect a special offering on the first Sunday of every month to support local or global economic justice, such as fighting hunger or providing assistance to underserved populations.

Yearly: Like most other Christians, Mormons celebrate Christmas and Easter. Unlike Christians in mainline denominations, the LDS do not celebrate Easter as part of a longer Holy Week observance, with services on Palm Sunday, Maundy Thursday, or Good Friday. Most Community of Christ congregations do observe the longer Holy Week. Community of Christ also promotes special themes for worship services during Advent, the four Sundays leading up to Christmas – another mainline Christian tradition that LDS have not adopted.

Some Mormons take note of Joseph Smith Jr.'s birthday (December 23) or the anniversary of his martyrdom (June 27), although those commemorations are not nearly as significant or widespread as Christmas and Easter. The martyrdom anniversary is the occasion for a yearly memorial service held jointly by the LDS and Community of Christ at Smith's grave in Nauvoo.

An important yearly tradition in Chris's life is "reunions" or "family camps." At these gatherings – a tradition dating back to the late 1800s – Community of Christ members from a region gather at a local campground, often owned by the church, to spend a week that mixes worship and Bible study with swimming, sports, and talent shows. In addition, Community of Christ organizes summer camps for children, teenagers, and young adults. Every four years, youth gather in regional meetings across the world called International Youth Forums. Chris has grown up looking forward to camps and family reunions as highlights of her year, and she now looks back on them as some of the most formative experiences in her spiritual life. Occasionally, she has witnessed at a reunion a continuation of the charismatic flavor of early Mormonism, as another attendee has felt moved to stand and speak "under the influence of the Spirit" to individuals or the entire gathering.

The LDS have no formal equivalent to Community of Christ reunions (although many LDS families organize their own *family* reunions). However, the LDS have a well-developed youth program. As teens, Lindsey and Logan attended "Especially for Youth" conferences, week-long events, often held on college campuses, that draw tens of thousands of LDS youth for motivational speakers and classes. In addition, Logan participated in the Boy Scout troop sponsored by his LDS congregation. The LDS have been a major supporter of Boy Scouts of America since the early twentieth century, although recently they have threatened to withdraw because of gay-inclusive policies. The LDS have not embraced the Girl Scouts program, but Lindsey has fond memories, including spiritual experiences, from attending church-sponsored Young Women camps in the summer.

For LDS, the church's General Conferences in Salt Lake City are an important semiannual event. LDS from around the world converge on the church's enormous conference center to hear sermons from the living prophets; elsewhere throughout the world, members might gather at their local churches to watch the proceedings by satellite, or they might watch in their own homes via the Internet. Community of Christ's World Conference, held every three years in Independence, has a similar significance as the venue where new revelations from the prophet-president are traditionally introduced to be voted on.

RITUAL AND THE LIFE CYCLE

In addition to marking the routine passage of time, rites mark turning points in the life cycle: transitions in a person's life, such as birth, marriage, and death. The LDS developed a more elaborate ritual life cycle than the Reorganization. Consequently, Lindsey's and Logan's lives have been more distinctive than Chris's, compared to what most Americans would regard as a typical upbringing. This illustrates one more way in which the LDS maintain a relatively greater degree of tension with the surrounding culture. However, there are some features common to both LDS and Community of Christ life cycles.

Birth and childhood: Mormons do not practice infant baptism. But shortly after birth, Lindsey, Logan, and Chris were each brought before their congregation during Sunday worship to receive a blessing. Lindsey and Logan were blessed by their father, Chris by one of the congregation's leaders.

Another childhood experience Lindsey, Logan, and Chris share is being baptized at age 8. That is the age at which early Mormons considered children old enough to be held accountable for their actions.

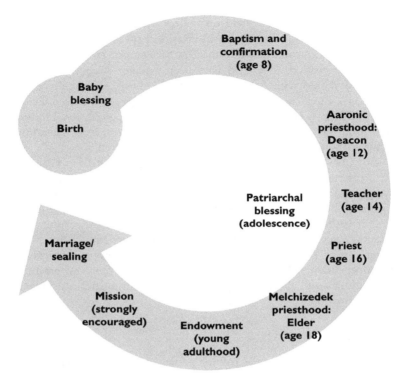

Figure 5.1 Logan's life plan: the ritual life cycle for an LDS male.
Image courtesy of John Hamer.

Adolescence: As an LDS male, Logan passed through adolescence by being ordained to successive offices in the Aaronic priesthood: deacon at age 12, teacher at age 14, and priest at age 16. At each stage, he took on additional ritual responsibilities. As a deacon, for instance, he distributed trays of bread and water to the congregation during the sacrament of the Lord's supper; once he became a priest, he was called on to read the prayers of blessing over the bread and water. At every stage – deacon, teacher, or priest – Logan belonged to a "quorum" composed of the other deacons, teachers, or priests in his congregation, with whom he attended Sunday religious education classes and Boy Scouts.

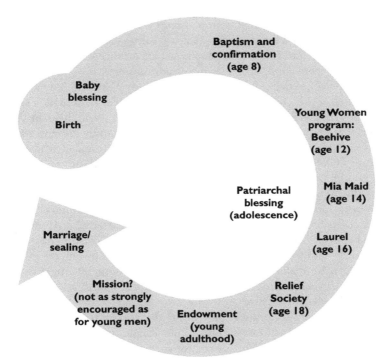

Figure 5.2 Lindsey's life plan: the ritual life cycle for an LDS female.

Image courtesy of John Hamer.

Lindsey was not ordained to the priesthood, of course. But she moved through a parallel religious education program for LDS young women, progressing through stages at ages 12, 14, and 16 as her brother had done. Lindsey's progress through the program culminated in her earning the Young Womanhood award, a medallion which she now wears in much the same way that other Christians wear crosses.

Chris's adolescence was not regimented in this way. Community of Christ congregations may have youth programs, but these do not have the uniform structure and stages that the LDS developed. In large part, this is because priesthood ordination in Community of Christ is generally reserved for adults, not teens. Nor was Chris's youth program segregated by gender, as Logan's and Lindsey's were.

While they were in high school, Lindsey and Logan each received their patriarchal blessing. This is a once-in-a-lifetime rite, which LDS look forward to as a special spiritual experience – a personalized revelation from God. The blessing is administered by a priesthood holder who has been ordained to the office of patriarch. The experience does not differ by gender; for convenience, we'll describe Lindsey's experience. Her blessing was a private event held in the patriarch's home, with only Lindsey's immediate family present. Laying his hands on Lindsey's head, the patriarch pronounced whatever words he felt inspired to deliver: promises about the blessings Lindsey would enjoy if she remained faithful and spiritual advice to guide her throughout her life. The blessing was transcribed and a copy was given to Lindsey; she will periodically reread it throughout her life, especially in difficult times or when she has to make major decisions.

The same rite is practiced in Community of Christ, where it is called an evangelist's blessing. (Unlike in the LDS tradition, the evangelist can be male or female.) However, the evangelist's blessing is traditionally linked to young adulthood rather than to adolescence. Chris decided to receive an evangelist's blessing while she was in college. While for Lindsey and Logan the patriarchal blessing was a once-in-a-lifetime experience, Chris can request an evangelist's blessing whenever she feels a need for special spiritual guidance.

Transition to adulthood: At age 18, Logan will be ordained to the first office in the Melchizedek priesthood, the office of elder. It is at this time that he will apply to serve as a full-time missionary if he chooses, in the end, to do that. As a missionary, he will spend two years living wherever the church decides he is needed; his family will pay his living expenses. From the time he was a young boy, Logan has been taught that he ought to serve a mission (although as many as two-thirds of LDS young men do not). Missions are meant to prepare young men for adult lifetimes of service as priesthood leaders. A mission thus serves as a rite of passage into manhood, analogous in some ways to military service in countries where that is mandatory.

When Lindsey turned 18, she was automatically enrolled as a member of the church's women's auxiliary, the Relief Society, which LDS women describe as a worldwide sisterhood. Because she is female, Lindsey did not grow up with the same expectation to serve a mission that Logan did. Historically, far fewer young women than men have served LDS missions. Until recently, young women didn't become eligible to serve until two years after young men, a policy that encouraged young women to marry instead. However, as of 2012 the minimum age at which women can serve has been reduced from 21 to 19, a change that led to an immediate surge in the numbers of young women applying to serve as missionaries.

An important ritual transition to adulthood for both LDS men and women is the endowment, the temple rite in which LDS solemnly covenant to follow God's laws throughout their lives. (See chapter 6.) Logan will receive the endowment shortly before beginning his mission. So will Lindsey, although if she didn't serve a mission, she would likely be endowed shortly before she marries.

Chris's passage to adulthood has not been marked in these ways. Since the Reorganization did not retain the Nauvoo temple rites, Chris will not receive the endowment. As described at the beginning of this chapter, Chris does have the option of serving in Community of Christ's World Service Corps, during which she would spend a summer performing service of some kind – but not proselytizing – somewhere in the world. Not many young adults in Community of Christ serve this kind of mission.

Marriage and maturity: Like most Americans, Chris expects that she will marry someday. But for Lindsey and Logan, marriage is more heavily weighted with significance. Retaining Joseph Smith Jr.'s Nauvoo-era teachings, the LDS view marriage for eternity as an ordinance essential for exaltation. If either Lindsey or Logan is still unmarried by the time they reach their thirties, they will be outside the norm for LDS life.

From the time they were children, Lindsey and Logan have been taught the importance of marrying in the temple – which means marrying within the LDS faith – so that their families will last forever. They could marry outside the temple, but that marriage would be "for time" only. An LDS couple might marry this way if, for example, their congregational leaders decided that one or both of them were not yet temple-worthy (were not adequately observing the church's standards). Once both were temple-worthy, they could then go to a temple to have their marriage sealed for eternity. A temple marriage can become an occasion for tension within the couple's families if some family members are not LDS, or if some who are LDS have been judged not temple-worthy; either way, those family members would not be admitted to the temple to witness the marriage ceremony. This problem does not exist in Community of Christ, where marriage is a public rite.

Once Lindsey and Logan marry and form their own families, the LDS life cycle will loop back onto itself, with a new generation being born to start the cycle over. Having been ordained an elder, Logan will be able to bless and baptize his children and ordain his sons to the priesthood, just as his father blessed, baptized, and ordained him. At some point in his middle age, Logan will probably be ordained to the office of high priest, making him eligible to serve in a greater range of leadership capacities in the church.

Chris might also be ordained to the priesthood as an adult, if she and her congregational leaders feel that God is calling her to serve in that way. Priesthood ordination is not as "automatic" in Community of Christ as it is for LDS males, who expect to advance through the various offices of the priesthood over the course of their lives, assuming they remain faithful to the church's standards. There is no expectation in Community of Christ that members, men or women, will necessarily be ordained. If Chris is ordained, she could be ordained to whatever office her church leaders judge appropriate – deacon, elder, priest, teacher – without having to progress through a series of offices, as in the LDS Church. She might hold the same priesthood office throughout her life, or she might be called to another office later on.

Death: In Community of Christ, death is marked with simple funerary rites, similar to what you would see in a Baptist or evangelical Protestant church (not the more elaborate ceremony of a Catholic mass). The service, held in a church or funeral home, will include tributes to the deceased, perhaps the deceased's favorite hymns, reference to Christian teachings about life after death, and a simple graveside service afterward.

LDS funerals follow this same pattern, but with a special additional act for individuals who have received the endowment. Those individuals will be buried in the biblical-like robes that LDS wear during temple rites. Clothing the deceased in temple robes is a service usually carried out by members of the person's congregation.

Another funeral rite practiced by the LDS but not in Community of Christ is the dedication of the grave by a Melchizedek priesthood holder. This happens as part of a graveside service and is typically done by a family member: Logan might be the one to dedicate his

father's grave, for instance. The dedication is a brief prayer blessing the gravesite. A traditional formula for the dedication prayer
blesses the site to remain undisturbed until the resurrection, when
the deceased will rise from the grave.

REGULATION OF MORMON LIVES

So far we've been looking at the *ritual* means by which Mormons
shape their lives: the rites that structure their experience of time and
the life cycle. In addition, various forms of *regulation* give shape to
Mormons' lives: regulations of diet, dress, and grooming; forms of
personal and institutional discipline; and ways of seeking revelation
to guide individual and group behavior.

DIET: THE WORD OF WISDOM

One of the widely known facts about Mormons (by which people
usually have in mind the LDS) is that they don't drink coffee or tea.
This fact is widely known precisely because it strikes many people as
odd. Why this prohibition?

Let's start at the beginning. Various social reformers in nineteenth-
century America offered advice about how to create perfect bodies
through health. Early Mormons developed their own health code
based on a revelation of Joseph Smith Jr.'s called the Word of Wisdom, which became part of Doctrine and Covenants, and thus part
of Mormon scripture, in 1835. The revelation advised Mormons to
refrain from "strong drink" (hard liquor) and tobacco (except for
medicinal purposes). Wine could be used for ritual purposes, notably
the sacrament of the Lord's supper; this was definitely wine, not grape
juice, which wasn't pasteurized until the 1860s. "Hot drinks" were
forbidden – hence no coffee or tea – but mild barley drinks, such as
small beer, were allowed. Eating meat was discouraged except during
the winter or in "times of famine and excess of hunger."

Smith's dietary teachings were tame compared to some of his
contemporaries. For example, Presbyterian minister Sylvester Graham, inventor of an early version of the graham cracker, advocated
complete abstention from alcohol, coffee, sugar, white bread, meat,
salt – and sex.

THE WORD OF WISDOM (EXCERPT)

Like many reform-minded groups in nineteenth-century America, Mormons developed dietary regulations intended to promote better health. The Mormon regulations were based on an 1833 revelation to Joseph Smith Jr. called the Word of Wisdom. Although Smith's preface to the revelation described it as a "principle with promise," not a "commandment," certain interpretations of the text have become important life-shaping norms for Mormons.

. . . [I]nasmuch as any man drinketh wine or strong drink among you, behold it is not good, neither meet in the sight of your Father, only in assembling yourselves together, to offer up your sacraments before him. And behold, this should be wine, yea, pure wine of the grape of the vine, of your own make.

And, again, strong drinks are not for the belly, but for the washing of your bodies.

And again, tobacco is not for the body, neither for the belly; and is not good for man; but is an herb for bruises, and all sick cattle, to be used with judgment and skill.

And again, hot drinks are not for the body, or belly.

And again, verily I say unto you, all wholesome herbs God hath ordained for the constitution, nature, and use of man. – Every herb in the season thereof, and every fruit in the season thereof. All these to be used with prudence and thanksgiving.

Yea, flesh also of beasts and of the fowls of the air, I the Lord hath ordained for the use of man with thanksgiving. Nevertheless, they are to be used sparingly; and it is pleasing unto me, that they should not be used only in times of winter or of cold, or famine.

Source: Doctrine and Covenants, 1835 edition, section LXXX (pp. 207–208). Available at josephsmithpapers.org. This edited excerpt retains the original punctuation, but long paragraphs have been divided for readability.

Early Mormons, including Joseph Smith Jr. himself, were selective in following the Word of Wisdom. The revelation had been presented to them as advice, not a commandment (albeit elevated advice since Mormons had accepted it as scripture). Mormons built breweries in Nauvoo, and Brigham Young advised all LDS migrating west to pack several hundred pounds of coffee. By the late 1800s, though, Mormons were becoming stricter about adhering to the Word of Wisdom, while simultaneously reinterpreting it for a new era. As the Prohibition campaign reached a critical mass of support across the United States, LDS embraced it and began to interpret the Word of Wisdom's ban on "strong drink" as a ban on all alcohol, not merely hard liquor. The LDS stopped using wine even in the sacrament of the Lord's supper, where the Word of Wisdom allowed it, adopting water instead. The Reorganization, equally committed to Prohibition, adopted grape juice, as many American Protestants did during this period.

By the beginning of the twentieth century, both the LDS and the Reorganization treated the Word of Wisdom as a ban on alcohol, tobacco, coffee, and tea. (In neither denomination did the Word of Wisdom's restriction on meat lead to significant support for vegetarianism.) In addition, both denominations had gone from treating the Word of Wisdom as recommended to treating it as mandatory, at least for some. For the LDS, Word of Wisdom adherence became a requirement for temple worthiness; in the Reorganization, it became a requirement for priesthood ordination although many unordained members adhered as well. For both movements, the Word of Wisdom became a symbolic boundary — something that adherents perceived made them distinctive from others. In reality, various other religious groups had distinctive dietary codes or a prohibition on alcohol, but what mattered is that Mormons *perceived* themselves as different. As medical science in the twentieth century discovered adverse effects of tobacco and caffeine, Mormons touted these discoveries as scientific evidence confirming Joseph Smith Jr.'s prophetic inspiration. These discoveries also prompted many LDS to add caffeinated colas to their list of forbidden beverages, although LDS church leaders refrained from making that position official. A tradition prohibiting caffeinated colas never developed in the Reorganization.

At the end of the twentieth century, another shift was evident in Word of Wisdom adherence. Although the Word of Wisdom remained a requirement for temple worthiness and thus an important boundary marking LDS identity, by the 1970s adherence to the Word of Wisdom in the Reorganization began to wane. The Reorganization's increasingly marginalized conservatives retained the Word of Wisdom as a boundary setting them apart from members who they perceived as becoming too liberal. But as the main body of the Reorganization turned into Community of Christ, congregations took on the custom, widespread among American Christians, of holding "coffee hour" in connection with Sunday worship – something that Lindsey and Logan might be startled to see. Community of Christ's official policy remains that no one who uses alcohol or tobacco products should be ordained; if Chris wanted to become a priesthood holder, she would need to abstain, at least in theory. In practice, though, this policy is often ignored.

DRESS: CLOTHING AND HAIRSTYLE

We mentioned that in nineteenth-century America, reformers promoted distinctive ways to eat. Some reformers also advocated changes in how people dressed – usually women's dress, often with the goal of promoting greater gender equality. Among some progressive American women of the 1800s, bloomers became fashionable: they were like pants, and thus more convenient to wear than dresses, but still traditionally feminine (frilly) and modest (puffy, not revealing the shape of the woman's legs). There was a little interest in this kind of thing among Mormons. The Strangites, a brief-lived faction that formed after Joseph Smith Jr.'s death, promoted bloomers. However, most Mormons in the 1800s resembled most other Americans in their manner of dress.

Some distinctive dress patterns emerged in the twentieth century. For the LDS, the distinctive pattern had to do with the temple garment. This was an undergarment that LDS donned for the first time during the endowment; this garment, they were told, represented the coat of skins that God gave Adam and Eve in the Garden of Eden, after they ate the fruit of knowledge and realized that they were naked. LDS were told to wear the garment as underclothing all their lives. (People owned multiple sets of the garment.) The garment set the standard for LDS modesty: it was to "cover their nakedness," implying that their other clothes had to be long enough to cover it. Also, the garment was meant to serve as a constant reminder of the covenants

LDS had made in the temple about living God's laws. Many LDS believed that the garment could miraculously protect them from physical harm as well.

The garment was initially like a union suit: single-piece long johns covering the entire body below the neckline, down to the wrists and ankles. In the 1800s, this style of underwear was not unusual. But by the early twentieth century, fashion and Americans' sense of modesty had changed. Wearing the garment now required LDS to cover their bodies in a way that was becoming notably conservative: they couldn't wear short sleeves or knee-length skirts. In the 1920s, LDS leaders accommodated these changes by authorizing a garment that had shorter sleeves and reached only the knee. The garment remained a single piece, however – unusual for twentieth-century underwear. The garment wasn't normally visible, of course, but LDS could become self-conscious about it in settings such as locker rooms; church publications offered advice about how to explain the garment to curious observers. Finally, near the end of the twentieth century, church leaders authorized a two-piece garment, with separate top and bottom. This change made the garment resemble a more conventional option for male underclothing: a white t-shirt and long undershorts. However, compared to what had become the norm for women's underwear, the garment looked anachronistic. LDS women wore knee-length drawers, couldn't expose their shoulders, and wore their bras *over* the garment top.

We have focused in this chapter on the LDS and Community of Christ, but at this point we should say something about the Fundamentalists. They did not accept the twentieth-century changes to the garment, retaining the nineteenth-century pattern with its even more demanding standards of modesty. Furthermore, some Fundamentalists – women especially – have retained styles of *external* dress and grooming that evoke the nineteenth or early twentieth centuries: hence the prairie-style dresses worn by FLDS women and their Gibson-girl style updos. The deliberately antiquated dress and grooming styles of these Fundamentalist women serve as a badge of difference from the world. They are advertising that they do not follow the world's changing fashions and that, unlike the LDS, they have not deviated from their forbearers' ways. Their very conservative image has the potential to symbolically counter assumptions about polygamy as licentious, saying in effect, "See how chastely we dress." On the other hand, the style can also reinforce outsiders' assumptions that Fundamentalist women are trapped in a patriarchal past and practice cultish conformity.

Meanwhile, the RLDS, having rejected the Nauvoo temple rites, have never used the garment. Their style of dress has always followed national norms.

The conservative tendencies of the LDS and the liberal tendencies of Community of Christ can be seen in how they typically dressed for church at the beginning of the twenty-first century. The LDS have retained a custom of wearing "Sunday best" at church. For Logan, that means a white shirt, dark suit, and tie. For Lindsey, it means a dress. Another sign of LDS cultural conservatism, post-1960s, is a distaste for beards. If Logan were to wear one, he would be practicing a kind of non-conformity; he wouldn't be allowed to serve as a missionary or an officiator of temple rites unless he shaved. As a teen serving in the Aaronic priesthood, Logan might not have been allowed to bless or pass the sacrament if he weren't wearing a tie. As for Lindsey, she would be signaling non-conformity if she wore a pantsuit to church. In 2012, LDS women advocating for greater gender equality in the church staged a "Wear Pants to Church Day" as a protest. Judging from the slew of online articles this event generated, something that seems like a small deviation to outsiders can register as a loud critique for culturally conservative insiders.

Chris dresses more casually for church, like most members of her congregation. In this, Community of Christ follows a broader trend in post-1960s American society toward less formal attire in worship. Americans of conservative temperament may regard this informality as a sign of irreverence; that's how LDS would be inclined to see it. But religious communities where informal dress has become the norm see it as a sign of their openness to everyone. Where Chris's father grew up wearing a white shirt and tie to church, and Chris's mother a dress, the family now wears business-casual blouses, polo shirts, slacks, even jeans. In this way, Community of Christ members critique their church's more conservative past. They are making a statement that they are no longer "uptight" about their faith.

DISCIPLINE: SELF-REGULATION AND INSTITUTIONAL REGULATION

All communities have ways to regulate the behavior of their members to ensure that community norms are followed, although some communities are more vigilant or demanding than others. The most effective regulation happens when members internalize the norms so that they follow them without the institution constraining them to do so – self-regulation.

In Mormonism, we see both self-regulation and institutional regulation. Self-regulation occurs as individuals develop an internal commitment to keeping their church's norms. Through instruction they receive at home and in church, they come to view themselves as having obligations to live up to: follow Jesus's teachings; keep God's commandments; make sacrifices of money, time, and energy to carry out the church's mission; develop their talents and God-given gifts. For LDS, the mandate to self-improvement is connected to Nauvoo-era teachings about exaltation: the LDS aim to progress to divine perfection. Their drive to self-improvement has inspired LDS to make prominent contributions to the larger American culture of self-improvement and efficiency – for example, LDS author Steven Covey's book *The 7 Habits of Highly Effective People*, or the Franklin day planners produced with great success by a Utah-based company in the late 1990s.

The drive to self-improvement can motivate individuals to impressive accomplishments, but it can also generate guilt or low self-esteem. In the 1980s, Utah news media called attention to a problem with depression among LDS women who felt that they were failing to measure up to God's expectations. Concern about this problem led to a softening in the church's language about the need to seek perfection and a greater emphasis on the teaching that Jesus's grace compensates for people's weaknesses – that God loves his children even when they fall short.

Institutional regulation can take various forms in Mormonism. The fact that church leaders control members' access to rites is one way in which leaders can hold members accountable for following the church's norms. In order to participate in temple ordinances, Lindsey and Logan need to hold a temple recommend; this in turn requires that they be interviewed every two years by local church leaders, who inquire about their religious beliefs, their observance of the Word of Wisdom and the church's sexual norms, and their tithe-paying. In all the Mormon streams, priesthood ordination requires those being ordained to attest that they meet the community's norms. In Community of Christ, priesthood holders are held to higher standards than unordained members. If Chris, for instance, were to be ordained, she would be expected to remain active in a congregation, tithe regularly, and make a life-long commitment to serving in office; as we noted earlier, she would also be expected, at least officially, to observe the traditional ban on alcohol and tobacco.

In the LDS stream, two other means of establishing accountability to the community are the institutions of "home teaching" and "visiting teaching." Every LDS household is assigned a pair of priesthood holders – home teachers – who are supposed to visit the household once a month, typically sharing a devotional thought and inquiring about the individual's or family's well-being. Logan has a home teaching companion with whom he visits another family in the congregation; Logan's father has his own home teaching companion and his own assigned family to visit; and then Logan's family receives a monthly visit from the pair of men assigned to be their home teachers. Visiting teaching is a parallel institution of women visiting women. Lindsey and her mother each has an assigned companion with whom she pays a monthly visit to another woman in the congregation; Lindsey and her mother likewise receive monthly visits from their visiting teachers. Home and visiting teaching are intended to ensure that every member of a congregation has a support structure as they face life's challenges. Women, in particular, may form close bonds with their visiting teachers. However, home and visiting teaching also provide a way for church leaders to "check up" on members. The practice can therefore be perceived as intrusive by members who are less active in the church, less committed to its norms, or more idiosyncratic in their beliefs.

The most intensive form of regulation in Mormonism is formal church discipline. From the beginning of the movement, Mormons aspired to be a holy community: the "pure in heart," as one of Joseph Smith Jr.'s revelations put it. Smith's revelations taught that in order to preserve the community's purity, members who seriously violated the community's norms should be expelled – excommunicated. A member accused of violations could be summoned before a church court composed of priesthood leaders, who would decide if the charge was true and if the sinner was adequately repentant to be allowed to remain in fellowship. During tumultuous periods of early Mormon history, church leaders at the highest levels were excommunicated on charges of disloyalty to the prophet.

Today, the three streams of Mormonism differ in how intensely punitive church discipline is. In Community of Christ, excommunication of members is virtually unheard of. However, priesthood holders who seriously violate the church's norms can be "silenced," a sinister-sounding term that means that the church revokes the person's right to function in priesthood office. In cases where silencing occurs, the relationship between the individual and the institution has typically broken down to the point that the priesthood holder leaves the church afterward. This occurred, for example, after the 1984 revelation that authorized women's ordination: priesthood holders who rejected the revelation were silenced and subsequently left to form their own organizations.

Among the LDS, excommunication is applied to individuals who are guilty of serious moral transgressions – an individual who lives with a same-sex partner, for instance, is likely to be excommunicated – as well as to individuals who are seen as publicly challenging the authority of church leaders. Cases of the latter sometimes receive media attention. For example, the 2014 excommunication of Kate Kelly, the leader of a group called "Ordain Women," drew national media coverage. Although the LDS Church still uses excommunication to enforce the community's norms, church leaders have become sensitive about outsiders' negative perceptions of the practice. Church officials customarily insist that discipline is not punishment but, rather, a loving attempt to help members bring their lives into harmony with Christ and his church. Excommunication means that a person is no longer entitled to participate in the church as a member: they could attend church meetings like any visitor, but they cannot participate in ordinances, and they are considered to have left the path that leads to exaltation. Excommunication nullifies, for example, a person's sealing to their spouse or other family members. If Logan were excommunicated, he could no longer bless or baptize his children, nor would he be able to attend family members' temple weddings. If excommunicated members later comply with the church's requirements, they can be rebaptized, and other ordinances they previously received, such as sealing, will be reinstated.

The most extreme forms of Mormon discipline have occurred in the Fundamentalist stream. We referred earlier in this book to Ervil LeBaron, who cited teachings about blood atonement to justify murdering members of rival Fundamentalist groups, as well as members of his own group who attempted to leave. The FLDS Church went through a period in the early 2000s when Warren Jeffs expelled community members who challenged his authority – expelling them not only from church membership but also from church-owned homes they had occupied under the FLDS version of the law of consecration. Around the same time, some 400 young men were expelled or voluntarily left the FLDS community for transgressions said to include talking to girls, watching television, or disobeying parents. Homeless and lacking job skills, these young men came to be known as the Lost Boys.

Although differing in intensity, all three Mormon streams have systems of church discipline to enforce their norms. These institutional forms of regulation, together with the self-regulation that Mormons internalize, provide a structure that helps sustain the distinctive shape of a Mormon's life – whether one views that structure positively or negatively.

CHARISMA: GUIDANCE THROUGH REVELATION

Mormonism teaches that as individuals make choices about how to live their lives, they can be guided by revelation. One form this can take is *personal* revelation, direct communication between an individual and heavenly beings. For a model, Mormons often look to the story of Joseph Smith Jr.'s First Vision. The story tells how the 14-year-old Smith went into the woods near his home – now called by Mormons the Sacred Grove – to pray for spiritual guidance; in response, he received a vision of the Father and the Son. Today, Mormons don't typically expect answers so dramatic. However, during the 1800s, it would not be unusual to hear a Mormon report receiving guidance from angels or the spirits of ancestors – perhaps in waking visions, perhaps in dreams.

Reports of visionary experiences became less common in the twentieth century within both the LDS Church and Community of Christ. This shift should be understood, in part, as a shift toward mainstream cultural values: in twentieth-century America, an individual claiming to have talked to an angel or an ancestor's ghost would tend to be regarded as weird, at the least. Mormons today are more likely to report receiving personal revelation in the form of powerful emotions or intuitions, which they understand as promptings from God's

Spirit. Such experiences can become the basis for a Mormon concluding that the Book of Mormon is true, or that God wants her to serve as a missionary, or that she should marry a certain man – or that God accepts her as gay, or that women ought to be ordained, or that Mormons should still practice polygamy.

There we see the difficulty that personal revelation can pose to Mormon communities where revelations authoritative for the entire faith community are also supposed to flow through prophets. If Lindsey decided that her personal revelation was telling her something that clashed with the teachings of the LDS Church's prophetic leadership, this would create a dilemma for her. Which revelation would she follow: her own or the leadership's? High-profile cases of excommunication are often the result of members following personal revelations that church authorities do not approve.

The challenge that personal revelation poses to institutional authority is another reason (along with Mormons having shifted toward mainstream attitudes about the supernatural) that personal revelation has become less dramatic in the largest and most stable institutions, the LDS Church and Community of Christ. It is potentially disruptive to institutional authority when individuals outside the leadership have visions or talk with angels. Over time, members have been discouraged from publicly discussing revelations of these kinds – on the grounds, for instance, that experiences so sacred should remain private. At the same time, the LDS and Community of Christ have developed bureaucracies that normally function not according to revelations received in the moment, but according to policy handbooks. Mormons still understand their churches as led by revelation; bureaucratic policies can be understood, after all, as divinely inspired. Nevertheless, bureaucratization represents a significant shift in how claims to revelation work within Mormon institutions.

Sociologists would call this shift "the routinization of charisma" and would see it as a recurring pattern in the development of new religions. In its earliest phase, a religion may be led by the charisma – the spiritual authority – of a visionary like Joseph Smith Jr., someone who claims dramatic or frequent revelations to guide the community. But, sociologists theorize, if a movement is to endure over time, visionaries with their potentially sudden innovations must give way to bureaucrats who systematize the movement's teachings and stabilize its procedures. In this way, spiritual authority within the movement becomes a matter less of personal charisma than of established routine.

None of the Mormon streams have gone so far in routinizing charisma as to declare that the time for revelation is past. All three streams insist that they are led by *continuing* revelation. But in the LDS Church and Community of Christ, the form that continuing revelation takes has changed. Joseph Smith Jr.'s revelations took the form of oracles. When the revelations say "I," readers are usually supposed to understand that the "I" isn't Joseph Smith; it's Jesus Christ speaking through Joseph Smith. By contrast, the prophets who lead the LDS Church and Community of Christ today do not deliver revelations in the form of oracles. The revelations most recently added to Community of Christ's version of Doctrine and Covenants are not couched in first person: there is no "I." Instead, these revelations read like theological treatises. In today's LDS Church, the prophets don't generate new sections of Doctrine and Covenants at all; the last LDS prophet whose words became a section of Doctrine and Covenants was Joseph F. Smith, the founder's nephew, writing in 1918. (As a result, Community of Christ's Doctrine and Covenants contains more revelations than the LDS edition and adds new ones more frequently.) When LDS leaders announced in 1978 that they'd had a revelatory experience prompting them to lift the black priesthood ban, the closest they provided to a written revelation was a memo announcing the policy change.

Continuing revelation in the form of oracles is found today only on the margins of Mormonism, often among groups who use those revelations to challenge the authority of the larger Mormon churches. In 2015, imprisoned FLDS leader Warren Jeffs issued a book of teachings and revelations, copies of which were sent to his followers as well as to Utah's mostly LDS state legislators. In the Reorganization tradition, a former member named Ronald Livingston has become the prophet of a small community in the woods of southern Iowa. In 2001, Livingston claimed to have translated a "sealed portion" of the Book of Mormon that Joseph Smith Jr. had not been permitted to translate. By producing oracles or translations of lost scripture, these marginal Mormon leaders reproduce the charisma of Joseph Smith Jr., thereby contrasting themselves to more mainstream Mormon leaders, whether LDS or Community of Christ, whose charisma is more routinized.

Whatever form it takes, continuing revelation helps Mormons adapt to a changing world. Mormons do not necessarily see themselves as bound to teachings and practices from their past. They understand certain principles as basic and unchanging, but they also expect new instructions to come in the future. Continuing revelation can produce dramatic change. It led to the suppression of polygamy in the LDS Church and to the ordination of women in Community of Christ. What Mormon lives will look like a hundred years from now is hard to predict because the concept of continuing revelation leaves Mormonism open-ended.

CONCLUSION

A Mormon life has a particular shape. Mormons have rites to structure their days, weeks, months, and years, and to mark transitions in the life cycle. Mormons have specific norms that regulate what they put in or on their bodies, mechanisms to regulate how group members behave, and understandings of how to authorize a course of action – that is, understandings of how revelation occurs. Other religious traditions have their own forms of ritual and regulation, which shape adherents' lives along other lines.

The shape of a Mormon life varies by stream: hence Chris's life differs from Lindsey's. And Lindsey's life differs from Logan's because the shape of an LDS life varies by gender. Compared to what passes as a "normal" lifestyle in American culture, someone in Community of Christ will experience less tension with the larger society than someone who is LDS. But the LDS are not the only contemporary Americans who pull back from certain cultural norms. There are other religious groups, too, who embrace ways of living that set them apart from the mainstream, either because they seek to preserve a minority ethnic or cultural identity or because they aspire to live by stricter standards.

At the risk of stating the obvious, we should note finally that while the lives of LDS and Community of Christ adherents are shaped by communal norms, thus allowing us to generalize about each stream, individuals within each stream may choose a path that puts them in higher or lower tension with those communal norms. Even in the stricter streams – the LDS and, stricter still, the Fundamentalists – no two Mormon lives ever look exactly alike.

SUGGESTIONS FOR FURTHER READING

Joanna Brooks, *The Book of Mormon Girl: A Memoir of an American Faith* (New York: Free Press, 2012).

Susan Buhler Taber, *Mormon Lives: A Year in the Elkton Ward* (Urbana: University of Illinois Press, 1993).

Lester E. Bush, Jr., "The Word of Wisdom in Early Nineteenth-Century Perspective," *Dialogue: A Journal of Mormon Thought* 14, no. 3 (Autumn 1981): 47–65.

Marie Cornwall, Tim B. Heaton, and Lawrence A. Young, eds., *Contemporary Mormonism: Social Science Perspectives*, 2nd ed. (Urbana: University of Illinois Press, 2001).

Douglas J. Davies, *The Mormon Culture of Salvation* (Aldershot, England: Ashgate, 2000).

Tim B. Heaton, Stephen J. Bahr, and Cardell K. Jacobson, *A Statistical Profile of Mormons: Health, Wealth, and Social Life* (New York: Edwin Mellen, 2004).

Armand L. Mauss, *The Angel and the Beehive: The Mormon Struggle with Assimilation* (Urbana: University of Illinois Press, 1994).

Colleen McDannell, "Mormon Garments: Sacred Clothing and the Body," in *Material Christianity: Religion and Popular Culture in America* (New Haven, CT: Yale University Press, 1995), 198–221.

Susanna Morrill, "Relief Society Birth and Death Rituals: Women at the Gates of Mortality," *Journal of Mormon History* 36, no. 2 (2010): 128–159.

MAKING HOLY PLACES

SACRED SPACE IN MORMONISM

Visit Independence, Missouri, a suburb of Kansas City, and you'll find, within an area of a few city blocks, more different Mormon groups than in any other spot on earth. At the center of this area, you can tour the towering Community of Christ temple, where retirees and young volunteers will tell you about their denomination's mission of peace and justice. Directly south of the temple, you can stop in at an LDS visitor center, where smiling missionaries will tell you about the saving ordinances of their church. Across a street to the west of the temple, you can walk across a grassy lawn, empty except for a small building that doubles as the congregational meetinghouse and visitor center of the Church of Christ (Temple Lot), so called because they claim to own the very parcel of land that Joseph Smith Jr. designated back in the 1830s for the building of a temple. This tiny group believes that the temple will yet be built at some future time.

Northeast of the Community of Christ temple sits a former high school, which now functions as headquarters for the Remnant Church of Jesus Christ of Latter Day Saints, a group that broke from the Reorganization in the 1980s over issues such as women's ordination. Walk a few blocks farther away, and you'll pass a non-descript house, the headquarters for an even earlier Reorganization breakoff: the Church of Christ (Fetting), who believe that John the Baptist visited one of their leaders in the 1920s. Directly across the street, you'll see the meetinghouse of the Church of Jesus Christ (Cutlerite), a modest building with a second floor where this very tiny sect performs temple rites. You wouldn't be allowed to witness those, but you could attend Sunday morning services on the lower floor, with a congregation that would number less than twenty – the Cutlerites' entire membership.

Independence is home to even more Mormon groups than the ones we've named so far. Within a mile of the Community of Christ temple, you could visit the headquarters or meetinghouses of half a dozen more groups. All of them want to be in Independence because of this site's sacred significance for them. In 1831, Joseph Smith Jr. identified this as the site for a holy city that would be the capital, the center place, for the kingdom that Mormons would build up for God on earth. Much as various Jewish, Christian, and Muslim groups want to establish a physical presence in the sacred city of Jerusalem, so various Mormon groups want to stake a literal claim in their sacred center place of Independence. In Jerusalem, friction between the different religious groups staked out there has at times become violent. That hasn't been the case in Independence. Still, a certain air of competition can be detected as the different Mormon groups assert to the others, if merely by their presence, their rival visions of Mormonism.

Many religious traditions treat certain places as "sacred." That means these places are set apart from everyday life. They hold a special status; they demand reverence. Sacred spaces may serve as the center point around which the group's mental map of the world revolves. They are places where people go to encounter gods or ancestors, places to seek healing or transformation. They provide gathering places, a sense of home or refuge. They announce a group's presence to the larger community. They can serve as physical reminders of a group's past, its stories and values. They can commemorate a group's accomplishments or its tragedies.

Sacred spaces are also sites of tension or conflict, within a group or with other groups. Sacred spaces are places where lines get drawn between the holy and the profane, between insiders and outsiders, initiated and uninitiated, privileged and unprivileged. They are places where struggles within and around a religious community are acted out: struggles for power or access, struggles over what the community should do or be, struggles over what place the religious community should have in its larger surroundings.

To be present, religions have to occupy space. So examining how religions occupy space shows us how religions work out the terms of their existence — how they literally *place themselves* in a society.

In this chapter, you'll read about:

- A bigger picture: sacred spaces in American religion.
- Sacred land in Mormonism.
- Sacred buildings in Mormonism: temples.
- Historic Mormon sites as sacred spaces and places of pilgrimage.

A BIGGER PICTURE: SACRED SPACES IN AMERICAN RELIGION

In this chapter, we'll focus on three kinds of sacred space: land, buildings, and historic sites. Before looking at how Mormons claim and use these kinds of spaces, let's establish some context by surveying sacred spaces in other American religious movements.

SACRED LAND

For some religions, particular pieces of land are sacred — not because a sacred building happens to stand on the land, but because the land itself is special. The example most familiar to most Americans (and important for understanding Mormon ideas about sacred land) is the Holy Land of Palestine, which is sacred to Jews, Christians, and Muslims because they all associate it with important figures from their traditions: Abraham, Jesus, Muhammad. For Jews in particular, the land's sacred character may be related to believing that God gave them a permanent claim to Palestine as their homeland.

Many religious groups immigrated to America from Europe, Africa, or Asia. If there's a land that's sacred to these groups, it isn't in America — it's somewhere back in the Old World. America doesn't have special significance in the ancient histories or myths of these religious groups for the obvious reason that these groups weren't in America until more recently. However, for *Native* Americans, tracts of land in America can have the kind of sacred significance that Palestine has for Jews, Christians, and Muslims. For example, the Black Hills of South Dakota are sacred to Lakotas because their myths say that it was there that their ancestors emerged from a lower world. Mescalero Apaches revere certain mountains in New Mexico as places where holy beings called the *gaa'he* live. In recent decades, Native Americans have struggled to regain control of lands they regard as sacred – suing to prevent commercial development of these spaces, or petitioning national park officials to respect sacred lands by closing them to visitors. But unless Native Americans own the lands they regard as sacred, their ability to regulate them in the way they deem appropriate is very limited.

SACRED BUILDINGS

Many religious traditions construct buildings they regard as sacred, typically because these are places of worship: churches, mosques, temples, and so on. When adherents enter these spaces, they may behave in special ways that indicate the building's sacred character: dressing in a formal way, bowing or crossing themselves, removing their shoes, covering or uncovering the head, speaking more softly or not at all. Access to certain portions of the space may be limited to certain people. Only priests, for example, may be allowed to approach the altar or the image of the god; or perhaps certain areas are reserved for men and others for women. These kinds of restrictions can give rise to conflict. For example, Jewish communities in the United States divided over whether or not women and men should be seated together during worship and then, later, over whether or not women should come to the pulpit to read from the Torah scroll.

Sacred buildings are important not only because of what happens inside them but also for how they're viewed from the outside. When a group constructs a sacred building, they're communicating a certain sense of who they are – traditional or modern, formal or informal, wealthy or poor. Sacred buildings announce a group's presence and assert a place in the community. Controversy can therefore erupt around the construction of sacred buildings if the group's presence is unwelcome to other members of the community. Since 9/11, for example, there have been protests in some American communities when Muslims have announced their intentions to build mosques. The most famous case was when Muslims set out to build a community center two blocks from the site of the 9/11 attacks in New York City. Protesters perceived the new building as an aggressive announcement of a Muslim presence – a slap in the face to those killed by Muslim militants on 9/11. By contrast, for supporters the building became a symbol that Muslims were welcomed as part of the American landscape – both the metaphorical social landscape and the literal skyscape of New York City.

HISTORIC SITES

Some sites become sacred because of things that happened – or are believed to have happened – there in the past. Methodists have "heritage landmarks" that preserve or commemorate early churches, colleges, or other sites associated with their movement's founding in the United States. Catholics maintain a shrine in Fonda, New York, where Kateri Tekakwitha lived, a Mohawk convert later declared a saint. By preserving and visiting such sites, members of a religious group pass on valued stories about their past to subsequent generations, as well as to outsiders. There can be tension or conflict around such sites if an event is remembered in different ways or if it has different meanings for different people. For instance, do the missions built by Spanish Catholic friars in California memorialize a noble pioneering and missionary endeavor, or do they exemplify the oppression of Native peoples?

Now that we've looked at examples from other religious traditions, let's look at different ways that Mormons have created these three kinds of sacred space – and what that shows us about different ways that Mormons have located themselves in America.

SACRED LAND IN MORMONISM

The first Mormons differed from other descendants of European immigrants in how they thought about America. Mormons were more like Native Americans in the sense that they understood America to be a sacred land. America was for Mormons the kind of place that Palestine is to Jews, Christians, and Muslims: a place where ancient events described in their scriptures had occurred, and a place where prophesies about the future would be fulfilled.

AMERICA AS A SETTING FOR ANCIENT SCRIPTURE

Around 600 BCE, according to the Book of Mormon, the family of a man named Lehi sailed to America after fleeing Jerusalem, which was about to be destroyed by the Babylonians (an event described in the Bible). In America, Lehi's descendants divided into two rival groups, known as Nephites and Lamanites. For a thousand years, they built cities and temples, founded colonies and kingdoms, conducted trade and waged wars. Then the Lamanites destroyed the Nephites in a genocidal conflict.

At the beginning of the twenty-first century, Mormons were increasingly divided in their ideas about where the events described in the Book of Mormon were supposed to have occurred, or if they had actually occurred at all. Some Mormons found it easier to accept the Book of Mormon as a literal history if they envisioned the Nephites and Lamanites as small groups living in a relatively small region – perhaps somewhere in Central America, or perhaps around the New York hill where Smith found the golden plates (dubbed by Mormons "Hill Cumorah"). But for most of Mormonism's history, the dominant view among believers was that the events described in the Book of Mormon unfolded across North and South America, and that the various Native American peoples were descended from the Lamanites. When nineteenth-century Mormon missionaries preached among Natives of North America, or among people of mixed Native-Spanish ancestry in Latin America, they presented the Book of Mormon as the lost history of their listeners. LDS missionaries who preached among indigenous peoples of the Pacific Islands, starting in the 1850s, became convinced that those peoples, too, were descendants of Lehi.

Mormons, then, regarded America as a second Holy Land. This was where ancient prophets had lived – prophets raised up by God among Lehi's descendants, whose teachings were recorded in the Book of Mormon. Even Jesus had walked in America, descending from heaven to visit the Nephites and Lamanites after his resurrection. America, Mormons believed, was a "land of promise," meaning that its inhabitants had a special promise from God that they would be blessed if they obeyed God's will.

Today, the idea of America as a sacred land remains more important among LDS and Fundamentalists than in Community of Christ – in large part because the Book of Mormon itself remains more important for the LDS and the Fundamentalists than for Community of Christ. Some affluent LDS tour ancient ruins in Central and South America with the understanding that they are touring Book of Mormon lands, in much the same way that people tour the Holy Land in Palestine. The membership of the LDS Church includes Native Americans, Latin Americans, and Pacific Islanders who believe that they are descended from Book of Mormon peoples and thus literally belong to the tribes of Israel, God's chosen people from the Bible. At times, this belief has fueled conflict between LDS of indigenous descent and white LDS leaders, with the indigenous LDS arguing for superior status based on their Book of Mormon ancestry. On the other hand, some white LDS in the United States interpret references to America as a land of promise to mean that the United States has a special place in God's plan for history. For these LDS, the Book of Mormon provides the basis for combining U.S. patriotism and religion in a distinctive way.

The Book of Mormon is not the only way that early Mormons linked American sites to events from ancient scripture. Joseph Smith Jr. taught that the Garden of Eden, where Adam and Eve lived, had been located in Jackson County, Missouri, where Independence is also located. Later Smith taught that another Missouri location, Spring Hill, was a place where Adam had met with several generations of his righteous descendants shortly before his death. According to Smith, the name of this place in Adam's language was Adam-ondi-Ahman. These teachings gave early Mormon settlers in Missouri a sense that they were living in the place where the history of the world began. Today, the site that Smith identified as Adam-ondi-Ahman is owned by the LDS Church; the site attracts LDS visitors, some of whom believe that a certain pile of stones is an altar built either by ancient Nephites or by Adam himself.

AMERICA AS A SETTING FOR FUTURE SACRED EVENTS

In addition to linking American sites with events from the ancient past, early Mormons linked American sites to prophecies about the future. The most important such site is Independence, Missouri. During the 1830s, Mormons gathered to Independence in order to build the New Jerusalem, which they also called Zion. Here they would greet Jesus upon his return to earth, which Mormons thought was imminent. The Mormons' Zion and the "old" Jerusalem in Palestine would be twin capitals from which Jesus would rule the world.

When the Mormons were expelled from Missouri, they pulled back to Illinois and built Nauvoo, but they still harbored the dream of returning to Missouri to build Zion. After Nauvoo collapsed, the LDS refocused their energies on building a kingdom for God in the Intermountain West, yet they envisioned a future day when they would "trek back to Jackson County" to build the holy city. That expectation persisted into the twentieth century. Meanwhile, the dream of resettling in Jackson County remained yet more vivid in the Reorganization, whose members lingered in the Midwest. By the 1920s, Joseph Smith III and a son who succeeded him had moved the Reorganization's headquarters from Illinois, to Iowa, to Independence, thus literally replanting the movement in its sacred center place. Many RLDS families relocated to Independence as well. Near the site where Joseph Smith Jr. had prophesied the building of a temple, the RLDS built a 5,000-seat Auditorium to house the World Conference, where delegates from around the world gathered to vote on church policy.

In the 1960s, a new revelation issued by RLDS prophet-president W. Wallace Smith called the RLDS to erect a temple directly across the street from the Auditorium, on part of a large plot of land that Joseph Smith Jr., W. Wallace's grandfather, had dedicated for that purpose. Completed in the early 1990s, the temple represented both the fulfillment of a long-held Mormon dream and a marked transformation of early Mormons' apocalyptic visions. The temple is understood by today's Community of Christ not as a sign that Jesus is coming soon to violently destroy the forces of evil, but as a symbol of the church's mission to promote peace and reconciliation in a divided world. The LDS, meanwhile, have pointedly not built a temple in Independence; when church leaders decided to construct a temple for that area, they placed it in nearby Kansas City. It would appear that LDS leaders view erecting a temple in Independence as a still-future project associated with Jesus's second coming.

SACRED BUILDINGS IN MORMONISM: TEMPLES

In addition to regarding certain lands as sacred, Mormons also developed the teaching that certain buildings were especially sacred – places where God's presence and power were manifested in a special way. Mormons called such a building a temple. A temple was more than a church, or meetinghouse. Mormons conceived a temple as a place where they could have unusually potent or direct encounters with God.

When Joseph Smith Jr. and his associates sketched plans for the New Jerusalem that the Mormons were going to build at Independence, they envisioned the city as having twenty-four temples at its literal center. These buildings were meant to be used not only for worship but also for spiritual instruction and church administration. In temples, Mormons would be filled with divine power so they could go out into the world to make converts, who would gather, first, to the New Jerusalem, and then, as the kingdom of God expanded, into satellite cities. Those cities would have their own temples, thus making them sacred places for people to live – places where people could live with God.

Because of the conflicts in Missouri, early Mormons were unable to build even one temple in Independence, much less twenty-four. The first Mormon temple was built, instead, in Kirtland, Ohio, in the mid-1830s. The building, which still stands today, had three floors, dedicated to different sacred purposes. The first floor was for public worship. The second floor was for a theological school. The third floor was for Joseph Smith Jr.'s office, meetings of the different priesthood quorums, and secular schooling. This temple was a major investment for the economically struggling Mormon community in Kirtland. They made that investment because Smith's revelations promised that in the temple they would be "endowed with power from on high." During the worship service to dedicate the completed temple, participants claimed to see angels; reportedly, an infant miraculously began to speak praises to God. Later, missionaries held a ceremony on the upper floor of the temple, during which they washed one another's feet (like Jesus washed his followers' feet) and were anointed with oil (like kings or priests, or Jesus himself, in biblical times). The missionaries believed that through this ceremony, they received an outpouring of spiritual power that equipped them to go out and preach to the world. In the Kirtland Temple, Smith had visions of Jesus, Moses, and Elijah. The LDS stream of the movement came to understand these visions as giving Smith authority to carry out certain aspects of God's work on earth, including the authority to seal marriages and families for eternity.

Mormon practices around temples entered a new phase in the 1840s, while the Mormon community was centered at Nauvoo. Here, too, Mormons constructed a temple, modeled in many ways after the Kirtland Temple. It had administrative office space, a large assembly hall for worship, even provision for a museum. But the emergence of new rites in Nauvoo changed how the Nauvoo Temple was used. Nauvoo's temple was the first temple in which Mormons performed baptisms for the dead, the endowment, and sealings.

BRIGHAM YOUNG EXPLAINS THE ENDOWMENT

The endowment is one of the rites performed in LDS temples. The endowment bestows sacred knowledge intended to be reserved for the faithful; for this reason, LDS are typically reluctant to describe the rite publicly. Detailed descriptions, photos, or tape or video recordings of the endowment are extremely offensive to most LDS – an act of desecration. However, Brigham Young explained the rite as follows in a sermon he delivered in 1853, on the occasion of laying the cornerstone of the Salt Lake Temple.

Be assured, brethren, there are but few, *very few* of the Elders [of the church], now on earth, who know the *meaning* of the word *endowment*. To know, they must experience; and to experience, a Temple must be built.

Let me give you the definition in brief. Your *endowment* is, to receive all those ordinances in the House of the Lord, which are necessary for you, after you have departed this life, to enable you to walk back to the presence of the Father, passing the angels who stand as sentinels, being enabled to give them the key words, the signs and tokens, pertaining to the Holy Priesthood, and gain your eternal exaltation in spite of earth and hell.

Source: *Journal of Discourses* (Liverpool and London: Latter-day Saints' Book Depot, 1854–1886), 2:31–32. Emphasis in original.

TEMPLES IN THE LDS STREAM

When the LDS migrated west, one of the first things Brigham Young did upon arriving in the Salt Lake valley was to dedicate a block of land for a temple. That temple became the literal center point of Salt Lake City, the "ground zero" from which streets were numbered moving out in the four compass directions (1st East, 2nd East, 3rd East, etc.). The Salt Lake Temple took over forty years to complete; in the meantime, the LDS built three additional temples in other western settlements. They were bringing to pass Joseph Smith Jr.'s vision of a sacred kingdom composed of satellite cities with their own temples. The importance of these temples for LDS religious identity can be seen in the way the LDS responded when Congress authorized the federal government, at the end of the 1880s, to seize the church's property as part of the effort to stamp out polygamy. Church president Wilford Woodruff explained to his followers that the prospect of the temples being confiscated was why LDS leaders had finally given in and suspended the practice of polygamy: God had revealed to Woodruff that the Saints *must* keep the temples in order to carry out their mission.

The first LDS temples in Utah, including the Salt Lake Temple, echoed the three-floor plan of the Kirtland Temple. However, the evolution of Mormon ritual in Nauvoo changed the way LDS used temples. Where the uses of the Kirtland Temple had included public worship, religious education, and training for ministry, the LDS moved those functions out of temples into meetinghouses. The rites of baptism for the dead, the endowment, and sealings became the entire function of the temple (with the exception of the Salt Lake Temple, which contains a large assembly hall and offices where the church's global leadership meet). Where the Kirtland Temple had remained open to the non-Mormon public, LDS temples are closed to the public after they are dedicated. By contrast, LDS meetinghouses, also called "chapels" or sometimes "stake centers," are open to the public. Meetinghouses are where Sunday worship is held; visitors are welcome, indeed longed for. But temples are open only to baptized LDS who present a recommend, signed by their local religious leaders, attesting to their worthiness, meaning that they tithe (donate ten percent of their income to the church) and observe the church's moral standards. Even the windows of temples are covered to obscure the gaze of outsiders. These are spaces set apart from the world outside. LDS understand this set-apartness as an expression of the buildings' sacred character. God is in the temple, and therefore a person must be worthy – spiritually prepared – to enter.

LDS downplay the exclusionary nature of this understanding of sacred space by insisting that anyone can enter the temple once they are prepared. But the practical, often painful, reality is that at any given moment, temple doors are closed to certain people: non-LDS family members, who cannot attend a loved one's marriage ceremony; LDS members whose temple recommends have been revoked because of church discipline; anyone with black African ancestry during the 130-year-long priesthood ban.

LDS temples vary in size and design, but certain features are constant. In the basement will be a baptismal font, large enough for two people to stand in, mounted on the backs of twelve sculpted oxen. (The Bible describes a similar basin as having stood in Solomon's Temple.) This is where baptisms for the dead are performed – underground, to symbolize proximity to the dead. Elsewhere in the temple there will be sealing rooms, each equipped with an altar where couples or families kneel to join hands for the sealing rite. It has become traditional to place mirrors on opposite walls of the sealing room such that when they reflect one another, they create the appearance of a corridor extending into infinity, symbolizing the eternal nature of a sealed relationship.

Until the middle of the twentieth century, LDS temples were equipped with a series of rooms through which participants moved as they received the multiple stages of the endowment. The rite began in a washing room – separate rooms for women and men – where different parts of participants' bodies were washed, anointed, and blessed. Men blessed men, women blessed women, an unusual exercise of priesthood-like authority on the part of LDS women. Those being blessed were then clothed in the temple garment, said to symbolize the coats of skins with which God dressed Adam and Eve in the Garden of Eden. Leaving the washing room, participants passed through rooms whose walls were covered with murals depicting the creation of the earth, the Garden of Eden, and the fallen world in which we now live. In each room, actors playing the parts of Adam, Eve, Satan, and heavenly beings performed successive scenes of an elaborate, symbolic drama that represented every man and woman's journey through life. The drama was interactive: as it unfolded, those watching made sacred promises that they would live by God's laws, including commitments to abstain from sex outside marriage, to be obedient to church authorities, and to dedicate their lives to building up God's kingdom. Participants put on robes that resembled priestly vestments from biblical times. They also learned "signs, tokens, and keywords" – hand clasps, gestures, and passwords that would enable them, in the next life, to pass by the angels who guard the way to the presence of God. The use of hand clasps and passwords resembled the ceremonies of Freemasonry; as in Freemasonry, participants in the endowment vowed not to disclose these sacred signs, tokens, and keywords to people who had not received the rite. At the end of the endowment, participants passed through a veil, or curtain, into a room decorated like a sumptuous parlor, representing their eternal home in heaven, where they would live with God.

The LDS continue to perform the rites of baptism for the dead, sealings, and the endowment, regarding these rites as essential for exaltation in the afterlife. Temples are the only places where these rites are performed, making temples supremely important for LDS. The endowment has evolved over time. One change is that since the middle of the twentieth century, live actors performing in multiple rooms decorated with murals have been replaced by a single room, like a small cinematic theater, where the drama is presented on film. This change has allowed the church to construct smaller temples, in turn allowing the church to construct a greater number of temples. Until recent decades, LDS living in some parts of the world would have to save for years to afford a single trip to a temple in their lifetime. By 2015, temples had become far more accessible, with close to 150 LDS temples operating around the world and more being constructed. Many LDS families have a portrait of their local or regional temple hanging in their home, often alongside wedding photos or family photos, symbolically linking their home to that sacred place, reminding themselves of the sacred commitments they made there. LDS are encouraged to attend the temple as frequently as they can, to repeat the rites in the names of individuals who died without receiving them. Thus LDS afford the dead the opportunity to be exalted, while at the same time temple-goers themselves can experience spiritual renewal and personal revelation as they sit in the unseen presence of God.

TEMPLES IN THE REORGANIZATION

By contrast to the LDS Church's 150 temples, Community of Christ has only two – the Kirtland Temple, now maintained as a historic site, and the Independence Temple. Community of Christ has no plans to build more temples. What accounts for this difference?

First, the Reorganization spent much of the nineteenth and twentieth centuries distancing itself from the LDS. This included distancing itself from the Nauvoo-era temple rites, which RLDS regarded as unnecessary at best, secretive and bizarre at worst. Second, the Reorganization remained more heavily invested in building up the area around Joseph Smith Jr.'s temple tract in Independence. Nevertheless, RLDS teachings about the significance of the hoped-for temple changed as the twentieth century progressed and RLDS leaders incorporated liberal Protestant ideals into their vision for the kingdom of God on earth. Rather than understanding the temple as preparation for the apocalypse or as a place to perform rites related to the afterlife, RLDS leaders came to see the temple as symbolizing God's "peaceable kingdom" – a better world to be created in the here and now.

Although the RLDS expected they would build a future temple at Independence, their vision for what they would do with it was undefined. Even when direction did come, it was vague. In the late 1960s, W. Wallace Smith presented a revelation stating that the time had come to begin building the temple but that the temple's functions would yet be revealed "from time to time." An addendum to this revelation assured the RLDS that "there is no provision for secret ordinances now or ever" for the coming temple. That is, there would be no baptisms for the dead or endowment ceremonies in the Reorganization's temple.[1] In the 1980s, W. Wallace's son, Wallace B. Smith, revealed that "the temple shall be dedicated to the pursuit of peace. It shall be for reconciliation and for healing of the spirit." The revelation went on to state that the temple would be a place for leadership education, for ministries "of wholeness of body, mind, and spirit," and a "place in which the essential meaning of the Restoration as healing and redeeming agent is given new life and understanding, inspired by the life and witness of the Redeemer of the world."[2]

In some ways, the new temple mirrored the purposes of the original Kirtland Temple. Completed in 1994, the Independence Temple housed the offices of the Reorganization's global leadership, as well as a seminary to train its priesthood. It housed a sanctuary where Reorganization members met for periodic conferences and public worship; also, a museum and archives. All of these uses of the temple replicated earlier uses of the Kirtland and Nauvoo Temples.

Yet the peace-and-justice focus of the Independence Temple was new, reflecting the Reorganization's realignment with liberal Christianity. To embody this new theology, a new ritual was instituted: a daily Prayer for Peace. At 1:00 every afternoon, temple staff and passing visitors gather in the temple's sanctuary for a short service, praying for peace in a different nation each day. Since the first Prayer for Peace in 1994, the ritual has spread to Community of Christ congregations across the world, many of whom incorporate it into their Sunday morning services.

The Independence Temple, with its distinctive 300-foot spiral steeple, holds great symbolic value in Community of Christ. Through streaming video, the prophet-president broadcasts an address to the church from the temple sanctuary every April 6, the anniversary of Mormonism's formal organization; this event spatially marks the temple as the center of the global church and temporally links the temple to the movement's birth, heritage, and future. The temple is a prominent element of Community of Christ's global "brand image," appearing on the cover of church publications as well as on key chains, mugs, and paperweights in the homes of members across the world, from Independence to India.

In many ways, the Independence Temple functions like a Christian cathedral: open to the public, a place for large meetings, a grand aesthetically pleasing structure. However, the fact that this temple stands in Independence, Missouri, on the plot of ground designated by Joseph Smith Jr. for the New Jerusalem temple complex, makes it more than a cathedral. The Independence Temple illustrates how the Reorganization maintains its Mormon heritage even as it has realigned itself with liberal Christianity.

TEMPLES IN THE FUNDAMENTALIST STREAM

Given how important temples were to the LDS, from whom the Fundamentalists branched off, you may be surprised that Fundamentalists have been building temples since only the end of the twentieth century. Rites that the LDS confine to temples, Fundamentalists have usually performed outside temples – most notably, the rite of eternal marriage. Some Fundamentalist communities have built structures called endowment houses in which to perform sacred rites, but these are architecturally modest and do not have as high a status as temples.

(During the 1800s, the LDS built endowment houses as a temporary measure until temples were completed.) Some Fundamentalists take the view that they will regain access to LDS temples at some future time when God sets the church back in order. Fundamentalists disapprove of changes that the LDS made in temple ritual over the course of the twentieth century. These changes include shortening the temple garment, lifting the black priesthood/temple ban, and rewording a covenant in which women used to pledge to "obey" their husband. (Now LDS women pledge to "hearken to the counsel" of their husband.)

Since the LDS lifted the black temple ban in 1978, a handful of Fundamentalist temples have been built. The Apostolic United Brethren have a temple in Ozumba, outside Mexico City; a tiny AUB breakoff has a pyramid-shaped temple near Modena, in southern Utah; and the FLDS erected a white limestone temple on their ranch in Eldorado, Texas. Law enforcement broke into the FLDS temple as part of the 2008 raid. While that temple's three-story structure recalls the temples at Kirtland, Nauvoo, and early LDS settlements in Utah, it's not entirely clear what the FLDS used the temple for. Reportedly, they built it expecting that Jesus was about to return.

HISTORIC MORMON SITES AS SACRED SPACES AND PLACES OF PILGRIMAGE

Many religious traditions across the world engage in pilgrimage – a journey to a place of sacred significance, which makes the journey itself a sacred experience. Mormons are no exception. In fact, Mormons may engage in pilgrimage, without calling it that, more frequently than any other group arising from American Protestantism. Every summer, hundreds of thousands of Mormons journey to sites associated with their movement's formative years, such as Palmyra, New York, or Nauvoo, Illinois. There they visit restored historic buildings and attend colorful outdoor pageants recounting the sacred events that occurred in these places.

If Mormons go on pilgrimage with great frequency, their pilgrimage practices do not exactly resemble those of other religions. For instance, many Catholics go on pilgrimage seeking healing or some other supernatural intervention for themselves or a loved one; Mormons do not typically visit their historic sites with that purpose.

Nevertheless, for Mormons, as in many other religions, pilgrimages are journeys that take believers to places where sacred exchanges occurred between humans and divine powers. By being present in these places, believers hope to access those same divine powers. Many LDS expect to feel God's presence ("the Spirit") while visiting a church history site, and they hope that the visit will strengthen their conviction (their "testimony") of the truthfulness of their church.

Around the globe, pilgrimage has dramatically increased in frequency and in number of participants since World War II. Conditions in U.S. society after the war helped make Mormons part of this global rebirth of pilgrimage. Middle-class Americans rode a wave of post-war prosperity and technological innovation that gave them more leisure time and mobility than previous generations. Mass ownership of automobiles, a new interstate highway system, a national park system, and disposable income meant that millions of Americans could become tourists and take family vacations. Among them were Mormons, both LDS and RLDS, who likewise took to the roads to see America. Some of the "sights" Mormons went to see were the "sites" of their religion's founding narratives.

The LDS Church purchased its first historic site in the early twentieth century: the jail in Carthage, Illinois, where Joseph Smith Jr. was shot. This became a kind of martyr's shrine, visited by LDS from around the country and staffed by LDS missionaries. In subsequent decades, the church purchased dozens of sites along the routes of nineteenth-century Mormon migration, from New England to California. These sites include Joseph Smith Jr.'s birthplace in Vermont; the Sacred Grove and Hill Cumorah in Palmyra, New York; early Mormon properties in Kirtland, Ohio, where the church has now rebuilt a nineteenth-century village; sizable portions of the Mormon settlement at Nauvoo, including a reconstruction of the temple there (which had been destroyed shortly after the Mormons abandoned the settlement); and landmarks along the trail that the LDS pioneers traveled to Utah. The LDS conceived of these historic sites as a missionary tool, to raise their church's visibility and provide venues for teaching non-Mormons about the faith. But in practice, the historic sites serve mainly to retell and embody a faith-promoting history to the already converted. The church has constructed temples at some historic sites, so that LDS can enhance their pilgrimage experience – performing the church's sacred rites in places with additional sacred meaning.

Much LDS pilgrimage is place-centered, meaning that the point of the pilgrimage is to experience a place of sacred significance. However, LDS have also practiced, especially in recent decades, what might be called journey-centered pilgrimage, where the journey, rather than the destination, is the sacred experience. In 1997, the LDS celebrated the 150th anniversary of the first LDS pioneer company's journey from Nebraska to Utah. In honor of that anniversary, several thousand LDS recreated the thousand-mile trek, driving horse-drawn wagons or pulling handcarts across the plains and mountains as their forebearers had done. Since then, LDS elsewhere in the world have reenacted the pioneer journey in their own locales. This activity has proved especially popular among youth groups, who miniaturize the sacred journey by pulling handcarts for a few miles and camping out for a night. Instead of retracing the actual route of the pioneers, these LDS transfer the sacred journey to their own location, whether that be western Massachusetts or Ulaanbaatar, Mongolia.

The Reorganization developed pilgrimage sites even earlier than the LDS. This was partly because the RLDS stayed in the midwestern and eastern United States, where much of early Mormon history occurred, and partly because some historic properties had remained in the hands of Joseph Smith Jr.'s descendants in the Reorganization. Among the properties owned by the Reorganization were Joseph Smith Jr.'s homes and gravesite in Nauvoo and the original Mormon temple in Kirtland. Like the LDS, the Reorganization placed guides at these sites who shared the message of their church along with the history of the site. Also like the LDS, the RLDS organized tour companies, youth trips, and family vacations to the sacred sites of early Mormonism.

In their efforts to distance themselves from the LDS, the RLDS used pilgrimage sites to advertise the differences between the two movements and to promote the Reorganization's sense of its own legitimacy. Take, for instance, the sign that the RLDS installed on the front of the Kirtland Temple for most of the twentieth century:

> The House of the Lord, Built by the Church of Jesus Christ of Latter Day Saints 1834. Reorganized Church of Jesus Christ of Latter Day Saints, In Succession by Decision of Court Feb. 1880.

The phrase "by decision of court" referred to a suit over ownership of the Kirtland Temple, which we recounted in chapter 3. RLDS believed that the court's decision had granted them legal recognition as the true heirs to Joseph Smith Jr.'s movement. The reality was more complicated than that, but the point is that the Reorganization used spaces like the Kirtland Temple to announce to the world that they were the real Mormons.

Because the LDS outnumbered the RLDS, most visitors to the pilgrimage sites owned by the Reorganization were LDS. Consequently, these sites became scenes of religious rivalry – as when, for instance, RLDS guides at Joseph Smith Jr.'s gravesite made a point of stating that the prophet was buried alongside his *only* wife, Emma (denying, in other words, that Smith practiced polygamy). Starting in the 1970s, however, the Reorganization emulated the professionalism of state-run historic sites, by contrast to the missionary-run sites of the LDS. This meant that the Reorganization no longer used its sites to challenge the LDS over who truly followed the founder. But the new approach alienated LDS pilgrims for a different reason: a visit to a Reorganization-owned site such as the Kirtland Temple felt more like a secular than a sacred experience. By the 2000s, Community of Christ had again shifted its approach to its historic sites: now it aimed to embrace both "the sacred and secular significance" of the sites and at the same time to promote "religious tolerance and open dialogue among all people." This approach reflected Community of Christ's alignment with liberal currents in American religion.

The fact that Community of Christ owns important sacred sites of early Mormonism ensures continued interaction with LDS and gives Community of Christ an outsized importance in Mormon culture. Small numbers of LDS who first encountered Community of Christ at its historic sites in Kirtland and Nauvoo have subsequently joined the denomination because they are attracted to its more liberal stances on women's ordination and gay relationships. Thus, somewhat unintentionally, Community of Christ's historic sites serve after all as a kind of missionary tool.

CONCLUSION

Mormons create and use sacred spaces differently than most Americans, although Mormon practices are comparable to those of certain other religious minorities. Like Native Americans, Mormons have regarded certain lands as sacred: Independence specifically, "America" more broadly. Mormons use the word "temple" in a distinctive fashion to designate a category of sacred building apart from churches or meetinghouses. While Community of Christ opens its temples to the public, the LDS and Fundamentalists restrict access to those whom church leaders judge worthy, a practice that outsiders may find secretive or exclusionary. Historic sites are another kind of Mormon sacred space; the significance these sites hold for Mormon pilgrims falls somewhere between the numinous intensity of a Catholic shrine and the more mundanely historical interest of a Protestant heritage landmark.

In common with sacred spaces of other religions, Mormon sacred spaces inevitably become sites of struggle. In these spaces, Mormons assert competing claims to authenticity or authority, competing understandings of the past or the future, or competing versions of Mormon identity. Each Mormon stream's way of creating and using sacred space expresses that stream's way of being in the world. Community of Christ seeks grounding in its Mormon heritage while reinterpreting that heritage along liberal theological lines: that project is materially expressed in the Independence Temple. The LDS aim to spread throughout the world while maintaining an identity that sets them apart from the world; they express that vision by constructing, around the globe, temples physically set apart from the surrounding society, open only to those who keep the church's standards. In keeping with their different theological focuses, Community of Christ's temple orients adherents toward working for world peace while LDS temples orient adherents toward family life and the afterlife. The fact that Fundamentalists have been slow to build temples is consistent with their sense of being in exile from the church, waiting for God to set things right. As some Fundamentalists become more assertive about proclaiming their legitimacy or living openly in society, it would not be surprising to see more Fundamentalist temples built. One way or another, Mormons will keep making themselves present and remaking their identities by making and remaking sacred spaces.

NOTES

1 Doctrine and Covenants 149:6a; 149A:6 (RLDS/Community of Christ editions).
2 Doctrine and Covenants 156:5 (RLDS/Community of Christ editions).

SUGGESTIONS FOR FURTHER READING

David John Buerger, *The Mysteries of Godliness: A History of Mormon Temple Worship* (Salt Lake City: Signature Books, 2002).

Craig S. Campbell, *Images of the New Jerusalem: Latter Day Saint Faction Interpretations of Independence, Missouri* (Knoxville: University of Tennessee Press, 2004).

John-Charles Duffy, "Concealing the Body, Concealing the Sacred: The Decline of Ritual Nudity in Mormon Temples," *Journal of Ritual Studies* 21, no. 2 (2007): 1–21.

David J. Howlett, *Kirtland Temple: The Biography of a Shared Mormon Sacred Space* (Urbana: University of Illinois Press, 2014).

Daniel H. Olsen, "Tourism and Informal Pilgrimage among the Latter-day Saints," in *Tourism, Religion, and Spiritual Journeys,* edited by Dallen J. Timothy and Daniel H. Olson (London: Routledge, 2006), 254–270.

Stephen C. Taysom, "Imagination and Reality in the Mormon Zion: Cities, Temples, and Bodies," in *Shakers, Mormons, and Religious Worlds: Conflicting Visions, Contested Boundaries* (Bloomington: University of Indiana Press, 2011), 51–99.

Ethan R. Yorgason, *Transformation of the Mormon Culture Region* (Urbana: University of Illinois Press, 2003).

GOING GLOBAL

MORMONISM'S INTERNATIONAL EXPANSION

If in 2015 you boarded a bus in Manila, Philippines, and rode for six hours to the north, you would arrive at the town of Binalonan. On the corner where the state highway intersects with a main town thoroughfare, you would see a stately concrete and brick building, topped by a steeple without a cross. The grounds surrounding this chapel are immaculately groomed; they also feature the nicest basketball court in the city, better than the one sponsored by the local government. This is an LDS chapel, as you might guess from the fact that it looks much like LDS chapels you've seen in the United States. With 700,000 LDS members in the Philippines, almost every town on Luzon, the Philippines' largest island, has an LDS chapel identical to the Binalonan chapel. In addition, the LDS are preparing to build their third temple in the Philippines – in Urdaneta, a town just a few miles away from Binalonan.

In contrast to the over half million LDS in the Philippines, the Community of Christ has only 1500 members in the country, making its presence far less visible than the LDS presence. In fact, if you didn't know where to look, you might not even know that Community of Christ existed in Binalonan. But it does. Pass the LDS chapel, zigzag down a few narrow residential streets, and you'll eventually arrive at a concrete chapel, built in the 1970s, on the grounds of a small church-sponsored elementary school. It's a simple building, but there's the logo that says "Community of Christ." Today, there's also a banner running down the side of the building to celebrate the anniversary of Community of Christ's founding. But this anniversary isn't the April 6, 1830, founding of the church in the United States. It's the March 13, 1966, "birthday" of the Reorganization in the Philippines, celebrated every year in Community of Christ's eleven chapels across the Philippines.

Both the LDS Church and Community of Christ were formally established in the Philippines in the mid-1960s. That era marked the beginning of a period in world history that many scholars call globalization. This is a period in which various processes – advances in communication and transportation technologies, massive flows of immigrants in multiple directions, the formation of international organizations and multinational corporations – have led to what one sociologist calls "the compression of the world and the intensification of consciousness of the world as a whole."[1] In other words, during the latter half of the twentieth century, the world became a smaller place. One of the many consequences of this change is that it has become easier for religions to "go global." Mormons have ridden the wave of globalization to expand into country after country since the 1960s. By 2015, the LDS had a presence in 175 nations and territories, while the smaller Community of Christ had a presence in more than fifty nations. More than half of all LDS and more than a third of Community of Christ's members now live outside the United States.

Mormon expansion overseas during the globalization era was greatly facilitated by the superpower status and technological superiority of the United States. Mormonism was one of many American-made "products" exported around the world, along with Coca-Cola, McDonalds, MTV, and Hollywood films. Like corporations seeking to market their goods in culturally diverse places, Mormons have had to work through the tension between *homogenization* (maintaining a consistent product and brand image) and *diversification* (adapting to different cultural preferences and expectations). In the case of Mormonism and other U.S.-based globalizing religions, that tension means grappling with a crucial question: To what extent, and in what ways, should the movement's teachings, practices, and institutions be adapted to non-U.S. contexts? As we've already hinted in our tour of Binalonan, the two streams of Mormonism that sought a global presence after World War II – the LDS and the Reorganization – devised different answers to these questions, resulting in different global churches.

In this chapter, you'll read about:

- A bigger picture: the globalization of American Christianity.
- A snapshot of Mormonism's global presence.
- The LDS strategy for globalization: correlation.
- The Reorganization's strategy: indigenization.
- Another bigger picture: three theories of globalization.

A BIGGER PICTURE: THE GLOBALIZATION OF AMERICAN CHRISTIANITY

American Protestants began sending missionaries to distant foreign nations in the 1810s – twenty years before the birth of Mormonism. American missionaries frequently aspired to spread not only Christianity but also "civilization," including American ideals of freedom and democracy. There was an economic side to all this: as some business-minded Americans of the 1800s pointed out, making people in other parts of the world Christian would be good for American trade, as these newly Christianized and civilized peoples would need Western goods. The convergence of missions, civilization, and commerce is dramatically illustrated in Hawaii, where American missionaries organized schools to educate native Hawaiian children, launched profitable businesses that enhanced their economic and political clout, and built up an American sphere of influence in the Hawaiian kingdom. Eventually, American missionaries helped to topple the native government and annex Hawaii as a U.S. territory.

By the late 1800s and early 1900s, Western imperialism and Christian missionizing had become closely linked across the world. In reaction, emerging independence movements in Asia and Africa criticized missionaries as part of these movements' efforts to break free of Western control. Indigenous protests against Western missionizing could take several forms. Some leaders worked to revitalize indigenous religions, as in India, where Gandhi revived Hindus' pride in their religion. Other groups rose up violently against missions, such as the Chinese who participated in the Boxer Uprising of 1899–1901, attacking missionaries and massacring Chinese Christians. Alternatively, colonized people might "take over" Christianity and do it their own way, as seen in the indigenous churches – churches led by native leaders, outside the control of foreign missions – that sprang up across sub-Saharan Africa around the turn of the twentieth century.

In the early twentieth century, a split developed between liberal and conservative American Christians over how to do missions. Liberals leaned more and more, as the century progressed, toward pluralist theologies: they saw religions other than Christianity as valid ways to live, and they therefore felt less of an impulse to make converts. Also, liberals felt "postcolonial guilt" about the human costs of Western imperialism. Consequently, liberals' foreign missions became focused on humanitarian aid and social justice – running schools and medical clinics, for instance – without actively trying to win Christian converts. Theologically conservative Christians did plenty of medical and educational work, too, but the goal of winning converts to Christianity remained preeminent in their missionary work around the world.

Meanwhile, a new form of Protestant Christianity, born in the United States, was experiencing massive growth worldwide. This new movement was Pentecostalism, which by the end of the twentieth century could claim half a billion adherents. Pentecostal churches, also called charismatic churches, embraced dramatic practices like faith healing and speaking in tongues, which they understood as outpourings of God's Spirit. Such churches were often founded by roving evangelists working outside the larger, older denominations. Nevertheless, as Pentecostalism expanded across the globe, its charismatic practices blended with many older forms of Christianity. Scholars have observed that in places like India, even Catholics have become, to some extent, "Pentecostalized" – that is, they seek dramatic outpourings of spiritual power.

By the end of the twentieth century, there were vibrant Christian movements in the global South – meaning Africa, Asia, and Latin America – which had initially been founded by Western missionaries but were now mostly independent of Western control. In fact, Christian churches in countries that had once received American missionaries, like South Korea, were now sending missionaries to the United States, which they saw as needing a Christian revival. At the same time that Christianity burgeoned in the global South, European churches declined, with the result that the global South became the numerical center for world Christianity. In the global

North – Europe and North America – older Christian denominations moved in liberal directions reflecting cultural trends in the West; but these denominations found that the churches that their missionaries had founded in the global South a century earlier did not want to follow.

For example: Every place in the world where the British established their empire, they also established Anglican churches, England's state religion – including in the future United States, where Anglicans renamed themselves Episcopalians after the American Revolution. Even after the collapse of the British Empire following World War II, Anglican churches worldwide remained connected as members of the Anglican Communion, which had 85 million members in places including Nigeria, Uganda, Zambia, South Africa, Australia, the United Kingdom, and the United States. However, when Episcopalians in the United States appointed an openly gay bishop in the early 2000s, many of their fellow Anglicans in the global South were appalled. The fight over homosexuality led to deep fissures within the Anglican Communion: Anglican churches in the global North tended to move, more or less cautiously, toward acceptance of gay relationships, while Anglican churches in the global South tended to oppose such relationships, more or less militantly, as contrary to biblical teaching.

A SNAPSHOT OF MORMONISM'S GLOBAL PRESENCE

How does the international growth of Mormonism fit into this larger picture of the expansion of American churches abroad?

Most LDS growth outside the United States has occurred since the 1960s, and most of it has occurred in the global South: Latin America, to be more precise. As of 2015, the LDS Church claimed roughly 6.5 million members in the United States and Canada, 6 million in Latin America, and 2.5 million elsewhere. With a little exaggeration, we could say that most of the LDS Church's growth outside the United States has occurred in American client states – that is, in countries that either used to be under American rule or are now closely tied to the United States, economically, politically, or militarily. This pattern would account for the church having flourished in Latin America, a part of the world where the United States

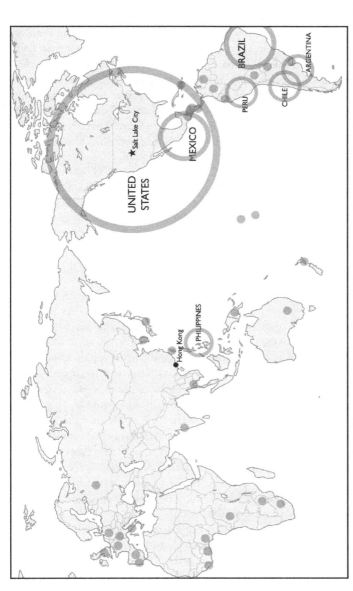

Figure 7.1 The seven countries with the largest LDS membership (as of 2010). Open circles represent the relative size of the membership in each country. Closed dots provide a rough picture of where else in the world the LDS have a significant presence.

Adapted from Brandon S. Plewe, ed., *Mapping Mormonism: An Atlas of Latter-day Saint History* (Provo, UT: Brigham Young University Press, 2012), 199. Adaptation courtesy of John Hamer.

has maintained very strong interests since the 1800s; it would also account for the fact that the largest LDS center in Asia is the Philippines, a former U.S. territory. Currently the LDS are growing rapidly in Africa, although their membership on that continent, less than half a million, is still relatively small compared to the rest of the world. The LDS have a numerically small but socially very significant presence in the island archipelagos of the South Pacific. According to the church's statistics, nearly half of all Tongans are LDS, and on most of the island nations, including Fiji, Samoa, and French Polynesia, the percentage of the population that is LDS is higher than the percentage of the U.S. population that is LDS (2 percent).

What about Community of Christ? It has only 200,000 members across the world, over two-thirds of whom live in the United States and Canada. However, Community of Christ has notable pockets of strength elsewhere in the world. Community of Christ's centers of growth outside the United States follow a different pattern than the LDS. The great majority of LDS growth outside the United States has occurred in the former Spanish Empire (Latin America and the Philippines), plus Portuguese-speaking Brazil. Community of Christ has tended to flourish in parts of the global South that are French-speaking, many of them places where the United States has had less impact, historically, than other Western nations. These places include French Polynesia (9,000), Haiti (11,000), the Democratic Republic of the Congo (11,000), and India (15,000; not French-speaking). In all the places just named, missionaries from the Reorganization began working before LDS missionaries; in the case of Haiti and the DRC, LDS missionaries weren't sent there until after the black priesthood ban was lifted, near the end of the 1970s. Meanwhile, in areas where the LDS have done well, such as Latin America, Community of Christ has only a skeletal network of small churches. When it comes to their percentage within national populations, Community of Christ members are numerically insignificant throughout the world – except in French Polynesia, where the Reorganization has been a notable religious minority since the late 1800s, today accounting for 3 percent of the population. Apart from French Polynesia, most of the Reorganization's growth outside the United States has occurred since the 1960s, the same as the LDS.

As for the Fundamentalists, they hardly register as a "global" presence. The most significant Fundamentalist communities outside the

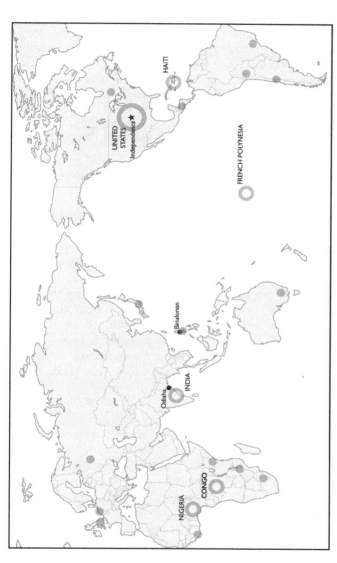

Figure 7.2 The six countries with the largest Community of Christ membership (as of 2010). Open circles represent the relative size of the membership in each country. Closed dots provide a rough picture of where else in the world Community of Christ has a significant presence.

Adapted from Brandon S. Plewe, ed., *Mapping Mormonism: An Atlas of Latter-day Saint History* (Provo, UT: Brigham Young University Press, 2012), 194. Adaptation courtesy of John Hamer.

United States are located *just* outside the United States, not far from the Canadian and Mexican borders. However, the Apostolic United Brethren have small groups in England, the Netherlands, and Germany. As a rule, Fundamentalists have not displayed a strong missionary impulse, whether for lack of resources or because they're reconciled to being (perhaps they prefer being?) the faithful few.

The Mormon streams differ not only in which parts of the globe they have flourished. They differ also in the policies they have pursued regarding homogenization and diversification. Let's hop quickly across several continents on a typical Sunday morning, to see how varied or how similar LDS and Community of Christ congregations can be.

SUNDAY MORNING ACROSS THE WORLD OF MORMONISM

Sunday is the usual day for congregational worship in the LDS Church. But in Hong Kong, a different LDS congregation meets for worship on every day of the week in a modest twelve-story building in the heart of the city. Local church leaders have worked out this unusual arrangement to accommodate the schedules of LDS hospitality-industry workers from the Philippines who work in Hong Kong. They rarely have Sundays off. In one small congregation of Filipino guest workers, nearly all the members are women; this necessitates placing women in leadership roles that men would hold elsewhere, although women still cannot administer the sacrament of the Lord's supper or preside over a meeting (since those are priesthood functions). The services in this branch are held in Tagalog, one of the two national languages of the Philippines. In another congregation, which meets in the same high-rise building on Sunday, men ordained to the priesthood exercise the usual leadership roles, although women may pray and testify during the services. This congregation is composed of Western expatriates – Americans or Europeans working in Hong Kong for universities, multinational corporations, or embassies. Their worship services are in English and are attended mostly by families with children.

Despite the variations among these Hong Kong congregations, the services themselves are very similarly organized. This similarity is not limited to Hong Kong: LDS worship is standardized across the world. All LDS congregations hold a three-hour block of Sunday services: one hour for sacrament meeting (where the congregation participates in the sacrament of the Lord's supper), one hour for Sunday School (for which men and women meet together), and then another hour for simultaneous meetings of the Relief Society (women only) and the priesthood quorums (men only). Across the world, all LDS congregations deliver the same Sunday school lessons; all sing translations of (mostly) the same hymns, typically to keyboard accompaniment; and all follow the same service procedures laid out by church headquarters in Salt Lake City. The dress of the men who preside over the services is the same across the world: white shirts and ties, preferably with dark suits. The people who fill LDS worship spaces across the world come from different countries, ethnicities, and social classes, and they speak different languages; but the worship structures they inhabit and the teachings they receive are standardized.

In contrast, Community of Christ services vary greatly across the world. On a Sunday morning in a rural village in the Indian state of Odisha, 100 people meet underneath an outdoor arbor covered with palm leaves. The service is led by a church secretary, a middle-aged man wearing a white Nehru-style shirt and white pants, who holds a microphone and makes announcements throughout the service. The men of the congregation sit on the ground on one side of the arbor, the women on the other. Children are everywhere. In fact, the entire village has come to the service. Not all are formally church members, since only those who reach age 18 and have been approved by a local church board may be baptized, but all consider themselves part of the church. These villagers are among several thousand Community of Christ members who live within an area of a few kilometers, all from the same tribal group: the Sora.

The congregation sings hymns in the Sora language, with religious texts put to familiar local melodies and accompanied by men playing drums, gongs, and other percussion instruments. A few people in the congregation sing from a small hymnal, but the booklet includes only words, not music. Halfway through the service, all rise to their feet and sing in unison the Lord's Prayer, the plaintive chant rising and falling almost like a Buddhist mantra. A lay teacher, a man in his twenties from another village who works as a farmer during the week, delivers a sermon based on a lectionary (schedule of Bible readings) that all Community of Christ ministers in the area carry.

The lectionary's cover features a photo of the temple in Independence, Missouri.

In Independence, on that same Sunday, a middle-aged woman is preaching on the same New Testament text, but in a very different setting. The woman is a local schoolteacher who, in the church, holds the office of elder. She preaches four or five times a year, in rotation with other congregation members who are ordained. Around sixty people, mostly elderly, plus a few families with children, are scattered around the pews of a brick church that was built in the 1950s. The service outline may vary from week to week, but it typically follows a "hymn-sandwich" structure familiar to many Protestants: hymns and prayers at the beginning and ending of the service, with a sermon in the middle. An element distinctive to Community of Christ is the Prayer for Peace: every week, the congregation prays for a different nation of the world, echoing a Prayer for Peace given daily in the Independence Temple. The hymns, accompanied by piano or organ, are sung in English, although occasionally the congregation may sing a verse in French, Tahitian, or Spanish, a gesture toward their denomination's international identity. Despite this self-consciousness about Community of Christ's global diversity, those who attend this particular congregation are all white. Within a 25-mile radius of this particular Independence congregation, one can count thirty other Community of Christ congregations, mostly the same size. Like many liberal Protestant denominations, the Community of Christ in the United States is graying but not growing.

How did two U.S.-based Mormon denominations come to look so different? How did the LDS Church become a movement that places diverse people in close proximity to each other while standardizing their religious identities? How did Community of Christ become a movement that loosely connects diverse peoples who practice very different localized forms of Christianity? The answer is that these two denominations adopted different strategies of globalization.

THE LDS STRATEGY FOR GLOBALIZATION: CORRELATION

The LDS Church's post-1960s global expansion coincided with the church's implementation of "correlation," a broad process of standardization in the church. Correlation takes its name from the

Correlation Committee, organized in 1960 by top-level LDS leaders. The committee was originally tasked with coordinating the religious education programs that had been independently developed by different church organizations: the priesthood quorums, the Relief Society, and the organizations for children and teens. However, the apostle placed in charge of the Correlation Committee, Harold B. Lee, had a more ambitious vision. He set out to restructure the entire church based on the ideals of standardization and efficiency that the Correlation Committee represented. The Correlation Committee became the model for many committees in the LDS hierarchy — a Missionary Committee, a Temple Committee, an Education Committee — all aimed at creating uniformity in church teaching and practice and a more centralized organization.

Lee looked to American corporations for models of how to organize his church more efficiently. The model corporation of the 1950s worked through committees, eliminated duplication of duties, and maintained clear hierarchies. These corporate traits appealed to Lee and other influential LDS leaders at mid-twentieth century. Through correlation, these leaders sought to make their church into the image of what seemed the most successful organization pattern of their era. They wanted the church to be able to do Christ's work more efficiently, at a time when the church was facing new organizational challenges created by a boom in its international growth.

What happened when correlation was implemented? Written resources for teaching LDS doctrines were shortened and the language simplified. This allowed church resources to be translated more quickly into the increasing number of languages used by LDS worldwide. Translations were made at church headquarters in Salt Lake City, not locally, to ensure a standardized church vocabulary. Church publications — leaders' sermons, Sunday School manuals, articles in church magazines, etc. — reiterated again and again the same basic beliefs and moral standards. This was done partly to ensure that church teachings and norms would remain consistent throughout the church's far-flung congregations. The goal was also to ensure that church publications could be understood by the most recent converts and by members with limited schooling.

Correlation standardized worship services and worship spaces across the world. It produced the standardized hymns, lessons, and three-hour block of church services we saw in our whirlwind

Sunday-morning tour of Mormon congregations. Correlation produced an LDS culture that favors homogeneity – hence the expectation that LDS men and teenage boys around the world will wear American-style formal dress to church: white shirts and ties. Correlation produced standardized architectural plans for LDS meetinghouses worldwide. This saved money and helped the church establish a recognizable brand image, but it also created some cultural oddities that some LDS cheerfully acknowledged. Gymnasiums with basketball hoops were a standard feature in LDS buildings, for instance, whether or not basketball was commonly played in that area. Pragmatically, LDS could see why this made little sense in Nigeria, where soccer was far more popular. Still, LDS meetinghouses exported basketball, a sport popular in LDS Utah (and among American missionaries), to the world.

Correlation standardized and improved missionary training. The church began to preach in the 1960s the expectation that its young men ought to serve missions. That expectation, coupled with the coming of age of the Baby Boom generation, led to an explosion in the number of LDS missionaries serving at any one time, from about 5,000 in 1960, to 30,000 in 1980, to 85,000 in 2015. After 1960, missionaries were required to work always in pairs and to wear the American-style formal dress that has become the trademark image of an LDS missionary: white shirt and tie for elders, long skirt (never pants) for sisters. The 1960s also saw LDS missionaries receive formal training, including language training, for the first time. Before that, missionaries had simply set off for wherever they had been called to serve. Now newly called missionaries spent one to three months in a training center, where they received intensive coaching, ten hours a day, on everything from how to speak Mandarin, to how to teach effectively, to how to smile when rebuffed.

GLOBAL STANDARDS *VS.* LOCAL PRACTICES: LDS AND DRINKING IN RURAL BOLIVIA

In this essay, anthropologist David Knowlton describes the difficulties faced by LDS men living in rural Bolivia. LDS norms require them to abstain from drinking to retain good standing in their church; cultural norms require them to drink on certain occasions to retain good standing in their community. Their dilemma exemplifies the tension that Mormons can encounter between global standards and local practices.

I have known Remigio since he was a teenager, and he is now in his mid-forties. He is a member of the LDS Church.

This morning, as most mornings of the fiesta, he is hung over. His face is drawn with anxiety and pain. What's wrong, I ask him. "At night, when I drink, I don't sleep. I walk the patio all night long. I feel a knot of pain in my stomach."

I thought he was going to describe a stomach ulcer or some problem with acid reflux. Instead he said the pain was "a feeling he had done something wrong."

The next day, late afternoon, Remigio is in the street with a couple of people. He is drunk, like you can only get from three days of drinking from dawn to well past dusk. He sees me and grabs my arm. "This is David. He is my friend. You are my friend, aren't you?"

I meet his companions, and he ushers me into the home. He says, "I am so happy. Yesterday Moises was here, you know. He stayed and got really drunk. We drank together. I asked him if I could get permission to build another story on to my house. For a long time now, when I ask for permission, they block me in the municipality. Moises said yesterday, since it is you, I will give you thirty days to do the construction. If you do it and finish it, we will not see it and you will have it. I am so happy. He will let me finish my house."

Moises, not his real name, is a prominent public official in the town, and he is a returned LDS missionary. I was not there when this conversation happened, but I was at the gathering earlier and Moises was drinking. Lest you think Remigio's drinking is unusual, let me note that almost everyone at the celebration was as drunk as he was. Remigio almost never drinks, but on feast days like this, when his family or close friends are celebrating, he feels enormous social pressure to drink, as does Moises. Copacabana is a town whose society is tightly integrated by feasts and obligatory drinking. To be anything but marginal requires drinking.

When we, here in the U.S., think of becoming a church member we think of a person in a voluntarist society, who is basically a free agent and can make choices about groups to belong to and identities to take on. On the whole, Bolivia is not that kind of society. For most people, becoming and staying an active LDS member means becoming marginalized by breaking ties with family, friends, and local society. Long-term, active members are those who have found the social support and inner strength to accept such marginalization and magnify it to find meaningful lives. Most people cannot find the inner and outer resources to succeed at this task. But that they do not manage to stay "faithful" does not mean that their Mormonism does not have meaning for them. I do not know if this is part of the knot of pain in Remigio's stomach, but I suspect it is.

Source: David Knowlton, "Ideas Post-Copacabana," *By Common Consent* (blog), February 19, 2009, bycommonconsent.com. Excerpted and edited for readability. Reproduced by permission of the author.

A CRITICAL LOOK AT CORRELATION

Correlation increased the power of top-level church leaders and decreased the autonomy that had been enjoyed by church organizations outside the priesthood quorums. This has meant decreased autonomy for women within the church, who created the Relief Society, the Young Women's program, and the church's programs for children. Once those organizations were subsumed under the standardized central hierarchy, the women who led and operated them lost some of their capacities for independent decision-making. Although correlation streamlined the church's structure in ways, it has also led to dramatic growth in the size and power of the central bureaucracy, much like the U.S. government ballooned in size during the twentieth century.

Correlation's concern to simplify church publications has led to religious education programs that members with longer experience in the church or greater amounts of formal education can find boring. LDS religious education, whether on Sundays or in the church's weekday programs for high school and college students, continually reaffirms basic beliefs; its goal is not to explore new ideas or new interpretations. Correlation restricts what the average LDS member in the world today is likely to learn of LDS doctrine and history. It's possible that many people who joined the LDS Church since the 1960s were never taught that God was once a man living on an earth, or that there is a Mother in Heaven, or even that Joseph Smith Jr. and Brigham Young practiced polygamy, because correlated materials often downplay or omit such ideas to avoid controversy. This creates a situation where LDS who learn about such subjects from non-LDS sources – increasingly easy to do, thanks to the Internet – may feel that the church has tried to conceal something.

Correlation is both a cause and a sign of conservative retrenchment in the LDS Church. As we've discussed throughout this book, the LDS steered a moderately conservative course through American culture after giving up polygamy. But that course became more decisively conservative during the second half of the twentieth century than it had been during the first half. Correlation gave leaders with more conservative interpretations of LDS religion the power to tamp down more liberal ones. Correlation appealed to LDS leaders not only because it promised corporate-style efficiency; correlation also reflected social and political proclivities among LDS leaders that made them distrust diversity. LDS leaders in the 1960s viewed the emerging civil rights movements in the United States with attitudes ranging from ambivalence to opposition. They expressed little support for anti-colonialist movements outside the United States and were less self-critical about exporting American religion abroad than were American Christians with more liberal leanings. Also, LDS leaders were standoffish toward the ecumenical movement, which promoted greater fellowship and cooperation among Christian churches; no LDS leader questioned the traditional LDS self-understanding as the one true church. All of these tendencies made correlation appealing to LDS leaders: it promised a unified church, free of the disorder that would be created by competing claims to power or competing visions of LDS identity.

By fostering international homogeneity among the LDS and orienting them toward American managerial culture, correlation made LDS susceptible to the charge that theirs was an "American church," a foreign export – something that some people did not welcome in their countries. During the 1980s, when the United States backed repressive right-wing governments in Latin America, LDS chapels in

South America were bombed, and some young missionaries killed, by leftist militants who viewed the LDS Church as an instrument of American influence in their countries. On the flip side, being associated with an American church may have appealed to some converts. Some people want to participate in a cultural institution associated with America or the West, much as some people in America and the West are attracted to religions they associate with "Eastern" or "indigenous" wisdom. The corporatized image of the LDS Church can suggest to potential converts that this is an institution where they and their children will learn values such as hard work and a disciplined life, can gain leadership skills transferrable to the workplace, or might find employment in the church's bureaucracy or religious education system. For some male LDS converts, donning a white shirt and tie is a way to materially reinvent themselves within their society. Then again, that way of dress can serve for critics as a symbol of American imperialism or of a globalized corporate culture that threatens to sweep away local customs.

So while the American image of the LDS Church was appealing for some converts, its appeal was limited and limiting. Correlation allowed the LDS to export their religion to the world as a standardized product. And if membership growth is a measure of success, then correlation was wildly successful – at least during the last half of the twentieth century. Since then, membership gains have leveled off. As the LDS Church moves into the twenty-first century, the majority of its members are neither American nor English-speaking; yet English remains the language of church headquarters, and the church's leadership at the highest levels remains almost entirely white American. (The most prominent recent exception has been Dieter F. Uchtdorf, a German serving in the First Presidency.) Although millions of LDS outside the United States are Latin American, not a single Latino has ever served in the First Presidency or the Quorum of the Twelve, the church's top governing bodies. Whether LDS outside the United States, or in it, will come to see this as a problem for their church's global identity remains to be seen.

THE REORGANIZATION'S STRATEGY: INDIGENIZATION

Leaders seeking to expand the Reorganization globally after World War II posed this question to themselves: How should they "translate" their message in a way that would reach people from many different cultures? A member of the Council of Twelve Apostles, Charles Neff, became a leading advocate for "indigenization." Neff assumed there was a core to the gospel that could be expressed in unique ways by any host culture. Furthermore, Neff envisioned the relationship between missionary and convert as mutual sharing, not as a one-way delivery of the gospel message by the missionary to the convert. Instead, people from different cultures should exchange cultural gifts that would create a new global church. Additionally, Neff and other RLDS leaders of this era thought that missionary work should not be simply about sharing a message; it should also be about improving the quality of life – the health and education – of the world's poorest people.

This vision was implemented by certain influential apostles who supervised missionary work outside North America, aided by younger church employees with similar ideas. The ethos of indigenization embraced by these movers-and-shakers at RLDS headquarters was popular in liberal Protestant churches during the same era; it was also promoted by progressive Catholics at the Second Vatican Council of 1962–1965. But support for indigenization at the top levels of the RLDS Church was not the only factor that contributed to this strategy's becoming entrenched in the Reorganization. At least equally important factors were the appeal of indigenization to new converts, the practical necessity for American leaders to trust local leadership, and the limited control that American administrators actually had in their mission fields.

Take the case of the thousands of Sora tribal members in India who joined the Reorganization in the 1960s and 1970s. Their encounter with the Reorganization profoundly changed their lives, which were already being reshaped by the forces of new markets and regional political structures reaching into their mountain villages in Odisha. But the Reorganization's emphasis on indigenization meant that the form of Christianity the Sora adopted only vaguely resembled the Christianity practiced by RLDS in the United States. Sora ended up practicing a form of Christianity that looked more like the dominant form of Christianity in their region: the Canadian Baptists who had operated in neighboring areas for more than a century. For instance, Sora organized congregational committees headed by an unordained church secretary who also presided over the weekly worship meeting, a form of church government common among nearby Baptists, but not practiced in the Reorganization elsewhere.

In converting to the Reorganization, Sora partially reinforced and partially transformed their tribal identity. In the late twentieth century, Sora people confronted a religious force that wanted to assimilate them: militant Hinduism. Nationalists, convinced that India ought to be a Hindu nation, encouraged India's tribal peoples to embrace a "proper" Hindu identity. Most rural Sora, however, had never thought of themselves as Hindu. By becoming a part of the Reorganization, Sora rejected reclassification as Hindus, which would have entailed classification at the bottom of a highly stratified caste system. Instead, Sora affirmed their pride in their tribal identity – by taking on a new religious identity. Allying themselves with an American church connected Sora to a *global* network, but it also helped them assert a distinct (non-Hindu) *local* identity.

The American RLDS missionaries who worked with the Sora had embraced indigenization. These missionaries assumed, therefore, that considerable parts of the Reorganization's American identity were irrelevant to the Sora's circumstances. Sora converts agreed. Sora selectively adopted and rejected aspects of the Reorganization as it had developed in the United States. They rejected the Book of Mormon, deeming it unnecessary, but they embraced – with modifications – the Reorganization's sacraments. For example, when the Sora held communion, they rarely read the prayers over the bread and wine that were prescribed in Doctrine and Covenants.

The strategy of indigenization spread through RLDS missions for pragmatic reasons beyond its appeal to converts. With a much smaller missionary force than the LDS, the Reorganization had to rely on local individuals to recruit more members in places like Nigeria and India. Hence most Sora converts to the Reorganization were evangelized by local Sora priesthood holders, and all missionaries who worked in the region for any extended time, whether or not they were Sora, were from India. Indigenous leadership was a practical necessity if the Reorganization wanted a serious international presence.

Today, Community of Christ's top-level leadership is more nationally and racially diverse than the LDS Church's. In 2015, the LDS Quorum of the Twelve Apostles was all-white and all-American – indeed, overwhelmingly born in Utah. In that same year, Community of Christ's Council of Twelve Apostles included a Canadian, a Briton, a Zambian, a Honduran, and a French Polynesian. (In another contrast to their LDS counterparts, five of Community of Christ's apostles, along with one member of the First Presidency, were women).

A CRITICAL LOOK AT INDIGENIZATION

The Reorganization's program of indigenization allowed it to expand at faster rates than the LDS Church in *certain* places, such as India or the Democratic Republic of the Congo. The Reorganization was more flexible about adapting to local forms of Christianity, while the LDS Church brought a less flexible program with an American flavor. However, the Reorganization's reliance on local leaders resulted time and again in the church allying itself with individuals who turned out to be religious "entrepreneurs" looking for a wealthy Western sponsor. These entrepreneurs developed enormous power at the local level, controlling the flow of resources from the American headquarters to the local people. Sometimes these local leaders pocketed funds and abused their power.

Indigenization brought about changes in the church back in the United States, as indigenization became a rationale that liberal RLDS leaders used to advocate for other theological reforms they wanted. When American RLDS leaders in the 1960s justified not teaching the Book of Mormon in India because it wasn't relevant to Indians, they sincerely believed that. But it was also true that the Book of Mormon wasn't relevant to these American leaders, either. They had come to doubt that the Book of Mormon was an ancient record, and their theological views were turning in directions aligned more with liberal Protestantism than with the Book of Mormon's more evangelical-flavored theology. These leaders therefore had their own reasons to nurture forms of RLDS identity that did not include the Book of Mormon.

In 1972, the World Conference debated how to deal with Sora tribal polygamy. The Reorganization had always staunchly opposed polygamy in order to distance itself from the LDS. But advocates of indigenization now favored accommodating polygamy as a feature of Sora culture. The World Conference finally adopted a policy that accepted polygamous marriages made before an individual's conversion but forbade entering new polygamous marriages after conversion. The debate introduced many American RLDS to a more relativistic understanding of their religion, which led some to question other teachings or practices that had been taken for granted in the church – such as the practice of ordaining only males. Indigenization was thus one force leading to the conservative-liberal split among American RLDS during the 1980s.

By the late 1990s, indigenization had precipitated an identity crisis of sorts in the Reorganization. How exactly was the church in the United States or French Polynesia connected to the church in Haiti or India? If the gospel was manifest in culturally appropriate ways everywhere while retaining its core essence, what exactly was that core essence? The diversity fostered by indigenization prompted leaders of the newly renamed Community of Christ to place a counterbalancing emphasis on common beliefs and values shared by church members around the world. Some Community of Christ members joked that this was their church's equivalent to correlation. However, the drive to establish "core values" or "enduring principles" in Community of Christ could never produce the same degree of homogeneity that the LDS Church had achieved. First, Community of Christ lacked the resources to create the institutions that LDS correlation had brought into being. Second, Community of Christ leaders were still committed to diversification. "Unity in diversity" became a catchphrase among leaders, with the implied emphasis on *diversity*.

That catchphrase has proved easier said than done. In the early twenty-first century, issues that had once preoccupied mostly American church members threatened to divide the global church. No issue illustrates this better than debates about gay inclusion, akin to the divide over this issue in the Anglican Communion, discussed earlier in this chapter. As Community of Christ members in the United States and Canada became increasingly accepting of gay relationships, some leaders elsewhere voiced urgent opposition – and did so in the name of indigenization. Haitians, for instance, claimed that the subject could not even be broached in their culture. Some Indians invoked the principle of indigenization to advocate a compromise: essentially, "Including gays and lesbians is an American practice; we have different norms in our culture." Then again, some French Polynesians suggested that traditional Polynesian practices, in which some men took on female roles and dress, anticipated changes only now taking place in the North American church. The crisis around gay inclusion in Community of Christ severely tested the merits of the indigenization model for all parties as they struggled to remain one global church.

ANOTHER BIGGER PICTURE: THREE THEORIES OF GLOBALIZATION

Having examined the different strategies for internationalization adopted by the LDS and the Reorganization, let's step back and relate those strategies to different theories of globalization – theories that seek to describe and explain global interconnectedness since the 1970s. We will highlight three prominent theories: McDonaldization, balkanization, and glocalization.

Some theorists see globalization as a process of "McDonaldizing" the world. By this, they mean a process of standardizing institutions, values, and practices around the globe. This has been a long process, starting in the Industrial Revolution and leading to a world that has become much more homogenous, as exemplified by the immediately recognizable McDonalds restaurants now found worldwide. McDonaldization values efficiency, calculability, predictability, and control. These are the values and organizing principles of modern corporations, but they have increasingly become the values and organizing principles of other kinds of structures, including government bureaucracies, educational systems, and religious institutions. Some theorists see McDonaldization as making institutions more accountable to the people they serve – the consumers. Other theorists have a darker view of the process: McDonaldization disempowers citizens by turning them into consumers, who are themselves products of the standardizing system. Furthermore, critics worry that McDonaldization obliterates diverse local cultures.

Other theorists describe globalization as "balkanization" or a "clash of civilizations." Balkanization gets its name from the Balkan peninsula, which during the twentieth century was repeatedly fractured as one national group fought another – Serbs against Bosnians, for instance. For balkanization theorists, globalization is a process of creating new blocs of power who are at war with each other. Major conflicts used to be fought between different nations: Britain against

France, the United States against Mexico, Japan against China. As a result of globalization, the world's major conflicts are now struggles on a larger scale over ideology, values, or religion – such as "the Islamic world" versus "the secular West." Balkanization theorists do not see globalization as a process of increasing interdependency, but a process of creating new fault lines of conflict between new adversaries.

Still other theorists think of globalization as a process of "glocalization," a word invented by combining "global" and "local." These theorists emphasize neither steamrolling homogeneity nor warring cultures. Instead, they see globalization as a process of combining aspects of different cultures to create new kinds of locally distinct cultures. For these theorists, globalization encourages new forms of local diversity as well as new forms of connection beyond the local level. The glocalization model sees cultures as constantly in flux, constantly being remade, constantly engaged in exchanges, though not necessarily equal exchanges, with other cultures. This model emphasizes ways in which local people selectively adopt, resist, or adapt cultural products from elsewhere. Take, for instance, Coca-Cola. McDonaldization theorists would emphasize that Coca-Cola is a standardized product with a standardized brand image worldwide. Glocalization theorists would emphasize the diverse ways that Coca-Cola is "remade" in local cultures – as when people mix it with other drinks, such as rum; or when people in some locales have become convinced that Coca-Cola has the power to cure wrinkles or revive the dead; or when some have claimed that Coca-Cola is a product of local origin, not an American invention. In short, glocalization theory examines how the global is constantly remade according to local preferences.

How do these theories apply to the creation of global Mormonisms? None of the theories fully accounts for how the LDS Church and Community of Christ have changed in the post-World War II world, yet each theory can be applied to some aspect of those movements' international growth. McDonaldization seems to describe correlation, LDS leaders' borrowing practices of American corporations to produce a church that is standardized across the world. Glocalization describes the diverse ways that members of Community of Christ in India, North America, and Haiti have developed for living what is supposedly a common gospel. And balkanization calls to mind the new fracture lines that are cutting across older denominational divides: when it comes to issues like gay acceptance, a liberal LDS minority have much in common with the majority of Community of Christ members in the United States, while most LDS in the United States would find that their moral views align with those of Community of Christ members in places like Haiti or Africa.

CONCLUSION

Although Mormonism was a missionary movement from its beginning – one of many American Christian movements that sent missionaries to distant places – Mormon denominations experienced their greatest growth outside the United States beginning in the 1960s. Different Mormon streams found their greatest missionary successes in different parts of the world. The LDS were most successful in places where the United States has had significant political or economic power; the Reorganization was most successful in areas of the global South that were less connected to American power.

The LDS and the Reorganization employed different strategies to project themselves abroad. The LDS, modeling their church's organization after a modern corporation, have exported a homogenized religion: standardized religious education programs, forms of worship, and norms of dress. The Reorganization, by contrast, encouraged local converts to diversify – to develop their own ways of teaching and practicing the religion, influenced by local Christian traditions. The LDS strategy, correlation, corresponds to the processes of globalization that scholars have called McDonaldization, while the Reorganization's strategy, indigenization, could best be described as a process of glocalization.

Each strategy brings its own challenges. Correlation has created a strong sense of unified LDS identity worldwide. But control over the crafting of that identity lies in the hands of the church's mostly American (also white) centralized leadership, as a result of which the LDS are often perceived as an American church. That image can attract converts, but it has also at times drawn antagonism, even violent opposition. On the other hand, the Reorganization's strategy of indigenization encouraged cultural diversity. But as a result of that strategy, Community of Christ has become something more like a network of regional churches, shot through with fault lines of difference that have created an institutional identity crisis.

* * *

Throughout this book, we've seen Mormons contending with larger currents in American culture. Like other religious minorities, Mormons had to find their place in a nineteenth-century United States dominated by Protestants who were leery of, or actively discriminated against, religious outsiders. Different Mormon streams – the LDS, the Reorganization, and the Fundamentalists – followed different paths through American society, with the result that some Mormons have experienced higher tension in relation to the cultural mainstream than others. How much tension they experience has depended partly on how Mormons define themselves to other Americans, and partly on how other Americans define them. In general, the Reorganization has experienced the lowest tension and Fundamentalists the highest, with the LDS steering a moderately conservative course somewhere in between. We see this pattern when we look at the Mormon streams' degrees of resemblance to the American Christian mainstream, their relations with the state, their practices around gender and sexuality, and other rites and regulations that shape adherents' lives. Despite persistent friction with evangelical Protestants around theology, today's LDS have much in common with evangelicals and other religious conservatives, who likewise live in some tension with mainstream American culture while nevertheless exercising important social and political influence. Community of Christ has much in common, at least in the United States, with liberals in the Christian mainline, who likewise experience less tension with mainstream culture but who are also graying and shrinking in the United States. Fundamentalists, meanwhile, live on the outskirts of American culture, where despite a climate of increasing religious tolerance they experience challenges common to other small or unusual religious movements that attract the pejorative label "cult."

Mormonism has changed in important ways over its nearly two centuries of existence. The controversies and shifts around polygamy are probably the most prominent example, but we can also point to the LDS black priesthood ban or to women's ordination and gay/lesbian acceptance in Community of Christ. The first Mormons' dream of building a holy city at Independence, Missouri, has been transformed – by the LDS, into an ongoing project of building temples around the globe for the performance of rituals that enable human beings to become divine in the afterlife; by Community of Christ, into a single operating temple at Independence, symbolic of that church's hoped-for unity and its mission to promote peace and justice on earth; by Fundamentalists, into little enclaves or half-hidden networks of adherents finding new ways to keep polygamous and communitarian ideals of the nineteenth century alive in the twenty-first. As Mormonism continues to expand outside its original American context, it will continue to change and diversify – more or less freely – as Mormons in new local settings contend with new cultural currents. This is bound to create new tensions, whether within each Mormon stream or in relation to outsiders. That is the way of all religious traditions.

NOTE

1 Roland Robertson, *Globalization: Social Theory and Global Culture* (Thousand Oaks, CA: SAGE, 1992), 8.

SUGGESTIONS FOR FURTHER READING

Matthew Bolton, *Apostle of the Poor: The Life and Work of Missionary and Humanitarian, Charles D. Neff* (Independence, MO: John Whitmer Books, 2005).

John-Charles Duffy and Hugo Olaiz, "Correlated Praise: The Development of the Spanish Hymnal," *Dialogue: A Journal of Mormon Thought* 35, no. 2 (Summer 2002): 89–113.

Global Mormonism Project, globalmormonism.byu.edu

Laurie F. Maffly-Kipp and Reid L. Neilson, eds., *Proclamation to the People: Nineteenth-Century Mormonism and the Pacific Basin Frontier* (Salt Lake City: University of Utah Press, 2008).

Armand L. Mauss, ed., *Dialogue: A Journal of Mormon Thought* 29, no. 1 (Spring 1996). Special issue on LDS expansion outside North America.

Brandon S. Plewe, ed., *Mapping Mormonism: An Atlas of Latter-day Saint History* (Provo, UT: Brigham Young University Press, 2014).

Gregory A. Prince and Wm. Robert Wright, *David O. McKay and the Rise of Modern Mormonism* (Salt Lake City: University of Utah Press, 2005).

Russell W. Stevenson, *For the Cause of Righteousness: A Global History of Blacks and Mormonism, 1830–2013* (Salt Lake City: Greg Kofford Books, 2014).

GLOSSARY

Aaronic priesthood: a subdivision of the Mormon priesthood; includes the offices of deacon, teacher, and priest.

Adam-God doctrine: a teaching of Brigham Young, asserting that God descended to earth to become Adam and that one of God's plural wives became Eve.

Adam-ondi-Ahman: a site in Missouri where, according to Joseph Smith Jr., Adam blessed his posterity in Bible times, and where he will someday reappear in connection with Jesus's second coming.

Apostles: a twelve-person council, originally serving as missionaries but later the second-highest level of administrators in the LDS Church and the Reorganization.

AUB: Apostolic United Brethren, a Fundamentalist Mormon group headquartered in Bluffdale, Utah, near Salt Lake City.

baptism for the dead: a Nauvoo-era rite in which a living person is baptized as a proxy for a dead person who did not receive Mormon baptism while alive.

blood atonement: a teaching of Brigham Young's era, that forgiveness for certain sins requires shedding the sinner's blood.

bishop: among the LDS, the leader of a local congregation, equivalent to a parish priest or pastor; in the Reorganization, a financial officer.

branch: a small congregation.

celestial kingdom: the highest level of the three-tiered afterlife envisioned by Joseph Smith Jr.; the realm where God lives.

center place: Independence, Missouri, the site of the future New Jerusalem.

correlation: LDS program started in the 1960s to streamline and centralize church governance, as well as to standardize teachings, policies, and meetinghouse architecture.

Cumorah: name that early Mormons gave to the hill in New York where Joseph Smith Jr. said he found the golden plates from which he translated the Book of Mormon.

Doctrine and Covenants: volume of scripture containing revelations to Joseph Smith Jr. and subsequent prophet-presidents. LDS and Reorganization editions have different contents.

endowment: a rite in the LDS and Fundamentalist streams, during which participants covenant to live by God's laws and receive sacred knowledge preparing them for exaltation.

exaltation: In Nauvoo-era Mormon teaching, progression to the state of Godhood in the afterlife; the ultimate goal for LDS and Fundamentalists.

Fast Sunday: Among LDS, the first Sunday of each month, on which LDS skip two meals and make a donation to the church's program to help the poor.

First Presidency: the highest-ranking leadership council in the LDS Church and the Reorganization; consists of the church president (prophet) and two counselors.

First Vision: Joseph Smith Jr.'s first visionary experience, as a teenager. He later described it as a communication from the Father and the Son, instructing him not to join any existing church.

FLDS: Fundamentalist Church of Jesus Christ of Latter-Day Saints, headquartered in Hildale/Colorado City (formerly known as Short Creek), on the Utah-Arizona border. Probably the most widely known Fundamentalist Mormon group due to the notoriety of leader Warren Jeffs.

Fundamentalists: in the context of Mormonism, individuals or groups who continued to embrace polygamy after the early twentieth century, when the LDS Church had abandoned it. The term is also used more broadly to refer to extremists or militantly minded traditionalists in various religions (fundamentalist Christians, fundamentalist Muslims, etc.).

garment: the sacred underclothing worn by LDS or Fundamentalists who have received the endowment rite.

gathering: relocating to join a Mormon community; a frequent practice in the 1800s, associated with the dream of building Zion.

Independence: city in Missouri designated by Joseph Smith Jr. as the site of Zion, the New Jerusalem; Smith taught that the Garden of Eden had been located in the same area. Today, the headquarters of the Reorganization and many other smaller Mormon groups.

institute: LDS program of religious instruction for college-aged students, the equivalent of a campus ministry.

law of consecration: a principle for redistributing wealth to provide for the economic well-being of all in the community; led to experiments in communal property and church-owned enterprises.

LDS: Church of Jesus Christ of Latter-day Saints, the Mormon stream led by Brigham Young following Joseph Smith Jr.'s death. The largest stream of Mormonism, headquartered in Salt Lake City.

Melchisedec (*or* Melchizedek) priesthood: a subdivision of the Mormon priesthood; includes the offices of elder, high priest, seventy, patriarch (*or* evangelist), and apostle.

Nauvoo: Illinois city that served as the Mormon capital in the early 1840s. Rites and teachings inaugurated in Nauvoo divided the Mormon community: the LDS, and then the Fundamentalists, retained them; the Reorganization rejected them.

ordinance: term used by LDS and Fundamentalists for rites performed by priesthood holders. Ordinances include baptism, the sacrament (communion), the endowment, sealings, and health blessings (given to people who are ill).

patriarch (*or* evangelist): an office in the Mormon priesthood; called "patriarch" in the LDS stream, "evangelist" in Community of Christ. The function of this office is to provide blessings – words of counsel or guidance – to individuals seeking inspired direction.

Pearl of Great Price: volume of scripture used by the LDS. Its contents include the Book of Abraham, which Joseph Smith Jr. said he translated from an ancient Egyptian papyrus.

priesthood quorum: in the LDS stream, a group of men or boys who hold the same priesthood office (deacon, teacher, priest, elder, etc.). Each quorum meets for religious instruction for one hour during the three-hour block of LDS Sunday worship.

Proclamation on the Family: a statement issued by the LDS Church in 1995 on gender, marriage, parenting, and the need for governments to protect the traditional family.

Proposition 8: a 2008 referendum, supported by the LDS Church, that amended California's state constitution to ban same-sex marriage.

Relief Society: women's organization established in Nauvoo, then reestablished in Utah by the LDS; all adult LDS women are automatically enrolled as members. Relief Society serves more or less as a female counterpart to the men's-only Melchizedek priesthood quorums.

Restorationists: a term with two distinct usages: (1) A broad category of Christian movements, including Mormonism, that see themselves as reinstituting the original Christianity of Jesus, which they assert was lost over time. (2) RLDS conservatives who left the church around the 1980s and have formed several different small groups.

RLDS: Reorganized Church of Jesus Christ of Latter Day Saints, also known as the Reorganization; the Mormon stream led by Joseph Smith III. Headquartered in Independence, Missouri, the RLDS Church renamed itself Community of Christ in 2001.

sacrament: for LDS, the weekly rite of eating bread and drinking water in memory of Jesus's body and blood. For Community of Christ, eight rituals practiced by the church: baby blessing, baptism, confirmation, communion, marriage, ordination, evangelist blessing, and prayer with anointing oil for the sick.

Sacred Grove: wooded area near Palmyra, New York, where Joseph Smith Jr.'s First Vision is believed to have occurred.

sealings: in the LDS and Fundamentalist streams, rites that bind family relationships, most often husband–wife and parent–child, so that they can endure into the afterlife.

seminary: LDS program of religious instruction for high school students; often held very early in the morning, before school.

seventy: a priesthood office, traditionally dedicated to missionary work; in today's LDS Church, high-level administrators working under the apostles.

stake: an organizational unit comprising several congregations. The term is inspired by the image of stakes being used to anchor a tent; Community of Christ no longer uses the term, but the LDS do.

telestial kingdom: the lowest level of the three-tiered afterlife envisioned by Joseph Smith Jr.; a blissful – but imperfectly blissful – realm containing people whom conservative Christian theologies would consign to hell.

temple: a special kind of sacred building in Mormonism, higher in status than the meetinghouses used for regular Sunday worship. A temple's functions vary across the Mormon streams but may include church administration, religious education, revelation, or rites intended to provide a special outpouring of divine power.

temple recommend: certification required to enter an LDS temple; signed by local church officials to attest that an individual participates actively in the congregation, tithes, and keeps the church's standards for faith and morals.

terrestrial kingdom: the middle level of the three-tiered afterlife envisioned by Joseph Smith Jr.; said to contain less-faithful Mormons and honorable non-Mormons.

ward: an LDS congregation. The term originally referred to subdivisions of a city, which in LDS Utah settlements doubled as units of church organization.

Word of Wisdom: dietary code from Joseph Smith Jr.'s revelations; variously interpreted and enforced across the Mormon streams.

Zion: the ideal city that the first generation of Mormons intended to build in Independence, Missouri. Mormons apply the name also to any community or society built on holy principles, especially on the law of consecration.

INDEX

CPSIA information can be obtained
at www.ICGtesting.com
Printed in the USA
FFHW01n0606060918
48183029-51902FF

9 781138 020481